PRINCIPAL BUILDINGS and ROADS, 198

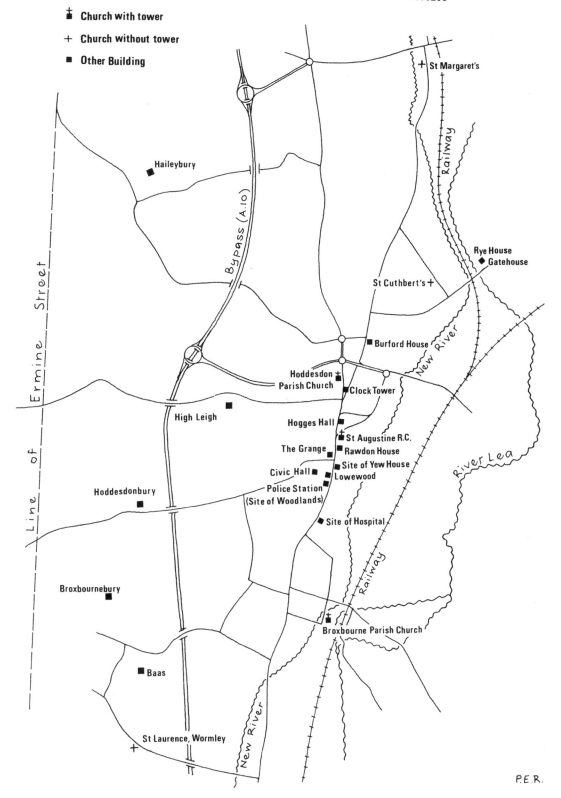

- ♯ Church with tower
- + Church without tower
- ■ Other Building

Haileybury

+ St Margaret's

Bypass (A.10)

Railway

Line of Ermine Street

Rye House
Gatehouse

St Cuthbert's +

New River

■ Burford House

Hoddesdon
Parish Church
Clock Tower

High Leigh

Hogges Hall

+ St Augustine R.C.

The Grange
Rawdon House

Site of Yew House
Civic Hall ■
Lowewood

Police Station
(Site of Woodlands)

Hoddesdonbury

River Lea

■ Site of Hospital

Railway

Broxbournebury

Broxbourne Parish Church

■ Baas

New River

St Laurence, Wormley

+

P.E.R.

HODDESDON
A HISTORY

Hoddesdon High Street looking south, 1891. In 1893 the post office transferred to its present building on the other side of the street.

HODDESDON
A HISTORY

SUE GARSIDE

Phillimore

2002

Published by
PHILLIMORE & CO. LTD
Shopwyke Manor Barn, Chichester, West Sussex, England

ISBN 1 86077 232 3

Printed and bound in Great Britain by
BIDDLES LTD
Guildford, Surrey

To Peter

Contents

List of Illustrations ix

Acknowledgements xi

Introduction xiii

I Early Days 1

II The Norman Conquest and Beyond 7

III Market Town 12

IV Elizabethan Hoddesdon 21

V Early to Mid-Seventeenth Century 31

VI Mid- to Late Seventeenth Century 44

VII Eighteenth Century 49

VIII Nineteenth Century – Hamlet to Urban District 58

IX Nineteenth Century – People and Places 77

X 1900-1974 – Urban District to Borough 90

Bibliography 107

Index 111

List of Illustrations

Frontispiece: Hoddesdon High Street looking south, 1891

1. Map of the area covered _____ xiii
2. Prehistoric animal bones _____ 1
3. Flint arrowhead _____ 2
4. Map of sites of Roman finds _____ 3
5. Roman pot _____ 3
6. Roman coarse ware vase _____ 3
7. Roman spearhead _____ 4
8. Samian ware shards _____ 4
9. Upper part of a quern _____ 5
10. Saxon spearhead _____ 5
11. Map showing the extent of the Danelaw _____ 5
12. Map showing pre-Conquest landowners _____ 7
13. Arms of Bassingbourne, Mandeville and de Bohun _____ 9
14. Hogges Hall, 1936 _____ 10
15. Map showing sites of manors _____ 11
16. Detail from map *c.*1570, showing the market cross and chapel _____ 13
17. Seal of Hoddesdon medieval hospital _____ 15
18. Arms of Ogard _____ 16
19. Rye House gatehouse _____ 16
20. Line drawing of the brass of John and Elizabeth Say _____ 17
21. Tomb of John and Elizabeth Say _____ 19
22. Tomb of William Say _____ 20
23. William Cecil _____ 21
24. Detail from map *c.*1570, showing southern Hoddesdon _____ 22
25. Arms of Thorowgood _____ 23
26. Page from the Thorowgood manuscript book _____ 23
27. Brass of John Borrell _____ 24
28. The *Salisbury Arms* inn, 2002 _____ 24
29. The *White Swan* inn, 2002 _____ 24
30. The *Bell* inn, 2002 _____ 24
31. The *Bull* inn, *c.*1960 _____ 25
32. The *Golden Lion* inn, 2002 _____ 26
33. The *Maidenhead* inn, 1872 _____ 26
34. Detail from map *c.*1570, showing the grammar school _____ 27
35. Detail from map *c.*1570, showing northern Hoddesdon _____ 28
36. Arms of Trappes _____ 30
37. The New River _____ 32

38. Map of the New River and a rival scheme _____ 33
39. Elizabeth Rawdon _____ 34
40. Detail of Rawdon family tree _____ 36
41. Sir Marmaduke Rawdon _____ 37
42. Rawdon House, 2002 _____ 37
43. Arms of Marmaduke Rawdon (later Sir Marmaduke) _____ 37
44. Thomas Rawdon _____ 38
45. Marmaduke Rawdon (the Traveller) _____ 39
46. Marmaduke Rawdon, son of Sir Marmaduke _____ 39
47. Shoes from the Grange _____ 39
48. The Samaritan Woman statue _____ 40
49. The old court house, built *c.*1610 _____ 41
50. The Market House, *c.*1826 _____ 41
51. Stanboroughs _____ 42
52. Arms of Bayley _____ 42
53. The *Thatched House* inn _____ 44
54. Constable's staff _____ 45
55. Settlement of the Poor document, 1728/9 _____ 46
56. Plan of Rye House, 1683 _____ 47
57. Friends Meeting House _____ 48
58. Document to the churchwardens and overseers of the poor, 1748 _____ 49
59. Map showing the position of almshouses and the workhouse _____ 50
60. Eighteenth-century fire pump _____ 51
61. Notice of prosecution of lawbreakers, 1791 _____ 51
62. The Clock House, *c.*1750 _____ 52
63. The Clock House, 1798 _____ 52
64. The chapel built by Robert Plomer _____ 53
65. Rear of St Catherine and St Paul's church _____ 53
66. The Grange, *c.*1960 _____ 55
67. The gates of the Grange, with details of monogram and pier _____ 55
68. Detail from a map of Hertfordshire, 1766 _____ 56
69. Lowewood, 2002 _____ 56
70. Rathmore House, 2002 _____ 57
71. William Christie _____ 58
72. C.P. Christie, *c.*1890 _____ 59

73. Christie & Co. stone beer bottle _____ 59
74. Christie & Co. stone jar _____ 59
75. Bird's-eye view of the brewery, 1897 _____ 59
76. Esdaile House, 1873 _____ 60
77. Esdale House, rear, 1906 _____ 60
78. Monument to Isabel Christie _____ 61
79. Rye House, 1784 _____ 61
80. The *Five Horseshoes* inn, *c.*1866 _____ 62
81. Bust of Queen Victoria and brass plate, Cottage Homes __ 62
82. Pamphlet for the re-erection of the Samaritan
    Woman, 1894 _____ 63
83. The pump which replaced the Samaritan Woman _____ 63
84. The High Street, 1811 _____ 64
85. The market house and the *Bull* inn, *c.*1830 _____ 65
86. The cattle market, *c.*1900 _____ 65
87. The Clock House, *c.*1830 and 1853 _____ 66
88. The police station in Lord Street _____ 67
89. The weather vane _____ 67
90. Lampits, *c.*1910 _____ 68
91. The watercress beds and the Lynch Mill, *c.*1890 _____ 68
92. The Coffin Houses _____ 69
93. Hoddesdon church and the National School, *c.*1850 _____ 70
94. Church re-seating plan, 1849 _____ 71
95. Hoddesdon parish church, 1880 _____ 71
96. Friends Meeting House _____ 72
97. Amwell Street, 1900 _____ 72
98. Boys' British School _____ 73
99. Boys' National School stone over doorway _____ 73
100. Foundation stone of Girls' National School _____ 73
101. Foundation stone of the Boys' British School _____ 73
102. The Girls' British School and the Congregational Church _ 74
103. Detail from 1898 Ordnance Survey map _____ 75
104. Rye House gardens, *c.*1910 _____ 76
105. Flyer advertising Rye House _____ 76
106. *Rye House Inn*, 2002 _____ 76
107. Lowewood and Borham House, 1964 _____ 77
108. John Warner as an elderly man, *c.*1850 _____ 78
109. Woodlands, *c.*1880 _____ 78
110. The Italian Cottage, 1898 _____ 79
111. The Coffee Tavern, *c.*1905 _____ 79
112. William Ellis as an elderly man _____ 80
113. Frontispiece of *Self Deception* by Sarah Ellis, depicting
     Rosehill _____ 80
114. Sarah Stickney Ellis _____ 81
115. Poem written by Mrs Ellis, 1846 _____ 81
116. Rawdon House _____ 82
117. Capsicum House cartoon _____ 82

118. High Leigh, *c.*1900 _____ 83
119. High Leigh Lodge and Pulham bridge _____ 83
120. Yew House, 1898_____ 84
121. Donat Henchy O'Brien _____ 84
122. Australian stamp depicting W.C. Gosse _____ 85
123. The High Street, from Stanboroughs northwards, *c.*1900 __ 85
124. Norris Lodge and Dr Bisdee, 1897 _____ 86
125. Montague House, 1861 _____ 86
126. The rear of the Grange, 1988 _____ 87
127. Brick inscribed with the name of A. Chittenden _____ 87
128. Burford House Academy, 1870 _____ 88
129. The building which housed the Middle Class Academy ___ 88
130. Terms and conditions of the Middle Class Academy,
     1880s _____ 88
131. Harriet Auber _____ 89
132. Christie's Brewery, *c.*1920 _____ 90
133. Advert for Christie's beer, Rye House, 1924 _____ 91
134. Flyer for the cinema, Burford Street, 1914 _____ 91
135. The Pavilion cinema and the brewery buildings, 1960s ____ 91
136. Plan of Rye House grounds, *c.*1925 _____ 92
137. Rye House, rear _____ 92
138. St Cuthbert's church, 1960 _____ 93
139. Works outing involved in bus accident near Hailey, 1913 __ 94
140. Advertisement for the Forres estate, 1936 _____ 94
141. Gardiner's advert, 1939 _____ 95
142. Front of *Hoddesdon Journal* with Nissen hut cartoon, 1939 _ 95
143. Library opening poster, 1937 _____ 95
144. Charles Giddings with the Samaritan Woman statue _____ 96
145. The Clock House, 1962 _____ 96
146. Hoddesdon parish church, early 20th century _____ 97
147. High Leigh Conference Centre _____ 97
148. Barclay Park lake, 1973 _____ 98
149. Beech Walk, 1962 _____ 98
150. National School buildings, 1972 _____ 99
151. Rawdon House sale document, *c.*1970 _____ 99
152. The Roman Catholic church, 2002 _____ 100
153. Woodlands, 1964 _____ 100
154. Hoddesdonbury, 1943 _____ 100
155. Aerial view of Hoddesdon, *c.*1960 _____ 101
156. The High Street, *c.*1950s _____ 101
157. The *Maidenhead* inn, *c.*1960 _____ 102
158. The High Pavement, *c.*1960 _____ 102
159. Aerial view of Hoddesdon, 1970 _____ 103
160. The High Street with the Tower Centre, 1970 _____ 104
161. Fourways, 1967 _____ 104
162. Crest of the Urban District of Hoddesdon _____ 105
163. The council offices _____ 105

Endpapers: Map of principal buildings and roads, 1988
              Map of the Urban District of Hoddesdon, 1936

Acknowledgements

Hoddesdon has been fortunate in having several local historians: Alexander McKenzie and Charles Whitley in the 19th century, A. J. Tregelles early in the 20th century, H. F. Hayllar and E. W. Paddick in the middle years of the 20th century and David Dent currently. I have drawn on all their expertise and am grateful to them. I am especially grateful to David for checking the manuscript, although, of course, any errors are mine alone.

I would like to thank my husband, Peter, for drawing maps, family trees and coats of arms; for his photography; and for all his help and encouragement.

Many thanks to Neil Robbins and Pauline Miller at Lowewood Museum for all their help; and to all the people who have donated photographs and artefacts to Lowewood which provide such a rich source of information and illustrations for the local historian. Thanks, too, to the staff of Hertfordshire Archives and Local Studies (HALS) and of Hoddesdon Library.

I acknowledge the following sources for use of their illustrations:

Lowewood Museum, Borough of Broxbourne: frontispiece, 2, 3, 5-10, 14, 21, 27, 31, 33, 47, 49, 50, 53-5, 57, 58, 60-3, 66, 71-7, 80, 82-4, 86, 87, 92, 95, 97, 98, 102, 107-10, 112, 115, 116, 120, 121, 123-5, 128, 130, 132-5, 138-45, 148-51, 153-63, endpaper, jacket illustration.

Hertfordshire Archives and Local Studies (HALS): 20, 23, 25, 26, 40, 43, 46, 68, 103.

Hoddesdon Library: 113, 114.

David Dent: 37, 79, 88, 90, 91, 104, 105, 111, 118, 136.

Peter Garside: 1, 4, 11-13, 15, 18, 19, 22, 28-30, 32, 36, 42, 48, 51, 52, 65, 67, 69, 70, 78, 81, 89, 96, 99-101, 106, 111 (inset), 119, 127, 129, 131, 137, 152.

A.J. Tregelles, *A History of Hoddesdon*: 39, 41, 44-6, 59.

St Catherine and St Paul's church, Hoddesdon: 64, 85, 93, 94.

National Philatelic Collection, Australia Post: 122.

East Herts Archaeological Society: 56.

Peter Rooke: Endpaper.

By courtesy of the Marquess of Salisbury: 16, 24, 34, 35.

By permission of the British Library: 17, 117.

All reasonable efforts have been made to find copyright holders for the illustrations used.

Introduction

✧

Hoddesdon

The name 'Hoddesdon' has been used for a thousand years and more, but what it has encompassed has varied over time. Hoddesdon has been a hamlet, a manor, a small market town, a parish, an urban district – firstly just consisting of one ward, then expanding to take in neighbouring areas – and is now part of the Borough of Broxbourne.

Choice of the area covered will therefore be somewhat arbitrary but, for the purposes of this book, Hoddesdon will be defined approximately as the area of the three northern wards of the Borough of Broxbourne, i.e. Hoddesdon Town, North Hoddesdon and Rye Park. This area is roughly from where Spitalbrook crosses the High Street in the south to St Margaret's Road in the north and from Ermine Street in the west to the River Lee in the east. Rye House is also included, although it stands just across the Lee in Stanstead Abbotts parish.

The name itself has been spelt in different ways. 'Hoddesdon' was Hodesdone, Odestone, Dodesdone and Hodesduna in Domesday Book and variously Hoddesden, Hodsdon, Hodsden, Hodestun, Hogsdon, Hogsden and Hoggesdon among others in subsequent records. Hoddesdon was not alone in this. Until spelling was standardised (and this only happened gradually during the 17th and 18th centuries as the amount of printed material increased), words

1 Map showing the wards of Hoddesdon Town, North Hoddesdon and Rye Park.

were spelt according to how they sounded to the writer. Another local example of varied spelling is Hailey, on the northern edge of Hoddesdon, which is known to have had at least 29 different spellings since the time of Domesday Book.

The first written record of Hoddesdon is in Domesday Book of 1086, which means that it was in existence at the time of the Norman Conquest. How long there had been a place called Hoddesdon is not known. The name is probably derived from a Saxon or Danish personal name – Hod, Hodda, Oddo or even Hogge. The suffix 'don' is Old English for a down or a hill, so the name presumably refers to a holding of land on the higher area beyond the marshy Lea valley bottom.

Because of the lack of written evidence before the 11th century no specific history of a place called Hoddesdon can be told, but an impression of the lives of those living in the region since the first people made their way into the Lea valley more than 10,000 years ago can be gleaned from archaeological finds.

Spelling of Names

Where variants in the spelling of family names occur, a single version is used throughout. For instance, for the Thorowgood family, this spelling is used, although Thurgood and Thoroughgood also occur in the records.

Either Lea or Lee can be used for the name of the river. The spelling Lea is used here, except where the modern navigation channel is referred to, when Lee is used.

Street Names

Some of Hoddesdon's streets have had different names in the past. The current names are given on the left.

Amwell Street	Ware Valley
Burford Street	Stanstead Valley
Conduit Lane	Honey Lane
Duke Street	Duck Lane
Essex Road	Marsh Lane
High Street	Fore Street (occasionally used)
Lord Street	Lord's Lane
Marsh Lane	Town (or Uptown) Marsh Lane

Monetary Conversion

Before 1971 money was reckoned in pounds (£), shillings (s.) and pence (d.). Up to the 17th century further divisions of the pound, nobles and marks, were also used.

Pre-Decimal

£1	=	20s.	=	240d.
		1s.	=	12d.

Nobles and Marks

£1	=	3 nobles	=	240d.
		1 noble	=	80d.
£1	=	1½ marks	=	240d.
		1 mark	=	160d.
		1 mark	=	2 nobles

Early Days

Prehistory to the Iron Age

During the Ice Ages Hertfordshire was too cold for permanent settlement. Over a vast period of time, perhaps a million years, the ice advanced and retreated. Water and ice laid down deposits of sand, gravel and clay. Neanderthal people hunted in the Lea valley area in periods when the cold was not so intense and the herds they depended on moved northwards.

When the ice finally retreated about 10,000 years ago at the end of four great Ice Ages and Britain began to warm, Mesolithic people moved from farther south to the newly habitable land. The Lea valley was deeper than it is today, the river was wide and fast-flowing with melt water, and trees began to grow more readily as the climate warmed. The Mesolithic people were hunter-gatherers and evidence has been found locally of their tools and camping areas. Their way of life changed very little over about 5,000 years and it has been estimated that about 4,000 BC there were perhaps a few hundred people living in the Lea valley in the stretch between Cheshunt and Hertford.

At about this time Neolithic people started to move northwards from Europe. These people were farmers. They cleared land of small trees and undergrowth for their crops and animals, and while they initially concentrated on areas with light soils, like the uplands of north Hertfordshire, it has been found that they cleared the gravel and boulder clay areas of east Hertfordshire from about 3,000 BC. Neolithic and Mesolithic people may have co-existed for some time because they were utilising different types of

2   From the top: horn cone of fossil bison, jawbone of woolly rhinoceros and mammoth's tooth, all found in the gravels of the Lea valley.

land – the incoming Neolithic farmers would have preferred the more easily cleared higher ground, leaving the wet valley bottom to the hunter-gatherers.

The introduction of metals from about 2,000 BC eventually led to more intensive farming methods. Copper and then bronze were brought in by traders or invaders and these metals were used in place of

3 Flint arrowhead found near Broxbourne church.

flint for some tools and weapons; but bronze (an alloy of copper and tin), although hard and durable, was expensive to produce. It was the introduction of iron in about 500 BC which made the most significant difference to farming. Iron ore was plentiful and axes and ploughshares could be made cheaply, allowing more woodland to be cleared and heavier soils tilled. Few traces of these early people have been found in Hoddesdon: a Bronze-Age occupation site and a coin of Cunubelin at different sites in the north of Hoddesdon; an Iron-Age/Roman site in Cock Lane; and a little pottery.

The Iron-Age people of Hertfordshire grew cereal crops and raised sheep, cattle and horses. The Celtish people of late Iron-Age Britain lived in warlike tribal groups. In the first century BC they were increasingly influenced by trade with the Roman Empire and by new ideas brought in by traders and refugees fleeing from its expansion. But it was not until Julius Caesar invaded in 54 BC that the people of Hertfordshire were directly affected by that expansion for the first time.

Caesar defeated Cassivellaunus (the overall leader of the Britons) at the crossing of the Thames and pushed on to seek out and destroy Cassivellaunus's capital. He met with resistance north of the Thames, perhaps in the Lea valley area. He pursued the Celts, laying waste to the land, burning and plundering. However, he did not have it all his own way. The locals employed guerrilla tactics: they drove their cattle away to safety to minimise opportunities of plunder; they mounted hit and run raids from the cover of the woods using chariots; and they picked off any Romans who strayed from the main force. The resistance was to no avail. With the help of tribes who had surrendered to him, Caesar eventually

located Cassivellaunus's base (the site of which is not certain, but was probably at Wheathampstead) and overwhelmed it. Terms were agreed, hostages were given and Caesar left Britain.

For the people of the Lea valley, this brief incursion by the Romans had lasting effects in terms of trade. Caesar's visit seems to have awoken traders from over the channel to the possibility of direct trading with areas north of the Thames instead of merely trading on the south coast. Flat-bottomed boats began to ply up the Thames and the Lea. The farmlands of Hertfordshire produced three of the commodities known to have been major exports from Britain: corn, cattle and hides.

Luxury goods were imported, but these would have been for the elite few. Most ordinary people lived very basically in farming communities. Their lives seem to have been fairly peaceful at this time. Small tribes had been absorbed into a large one, the Catuvellauni, which controlled a large area including what is now Hertfordshire. The banks and ditches surrounding farms served as fencing for livestock rather than as defences.

Roman Conquest

Roman legions landed in Kent in AD 43 and two months later captured Colchester. After this they met little resistance as they moved north and west. The Lea valley as far as Ware would have been too marshy for a large army to attempt an east-west crossing and anyway there appears to have been little disruption in Hertfordshire as a whole; it may be that there was sufficient pro-Roman sympathy for a smooth transition to a client kingdom to take place, with a native leader ruling on behalf of Rome.

The Boudiccan revolt of AD 60 centred on Colchester (Camulodunum), London and then Verulamium (St Albans). For people living in the Lea valley area within this triangle it must have been a terrifying experience, even though they were not directly involved in the carnage. After the upheavals of the revolt and Boudicca's eventual defeat, life slowly settled into a more peaceful routine.

Life in Roman Hertfordshire

The Roman road system in Britain was established soon after invasion because the Romans were well aware of the need to ensure the army's supply lines in a new province. Ermine Street was the great north road from London to York. It ran to the west of the Lea, passing through the woods above what was to be Hoddesdon, and crossed the river where it curves to the west at Ware. Trade increased even more as Britain became a stable province of the empire rather than an unpredictable foreign land. Ware became a prosperous town in the later Roman period, served by both Ermine Street and the River Lea. Agriculture was the main industry in Hertfordshire. Wheat was the most important arable crop, followed by barley. Of the livestock, cattle were most important. Pigs and poultry also provided common sources of meat. Pigs could be grazed in woodland areas and the heavy acid soils, such as the London Clay of south-east Hertfordshire, probably still had large areas of woodland.

No evidence of any sizeable Roman settlement or villa has been found in Hoddesdon, but a few artefacts have been found which indicate some presence of habitation, such as farmsteads, in the area. As well as farming, the making of baskets and rush matting may well have been a local industry. Given the marshy nature of the Lea valley, rushes and willows would have been plentiful.

Roman pottery has been found at several sites in Hoddesdon. Burial urns were found near High Leigh, and coarse pottery and bones in Pauls Lane. In 1874, while a new road, later appropriately called Roman Street, was being dug, a trench about 2.5 metres long was uncovered. It contained the remains of several Roman vases and both a Roman and a Saxon spearhead. In 1901 a bronze fibula (clasp)

4 Map of sites of Roman finds.

5 (below) Roman pot found when building Roman Street.

6 (bottom) Roman coarse-ware vase found in excavation in Roman Street in 1874.

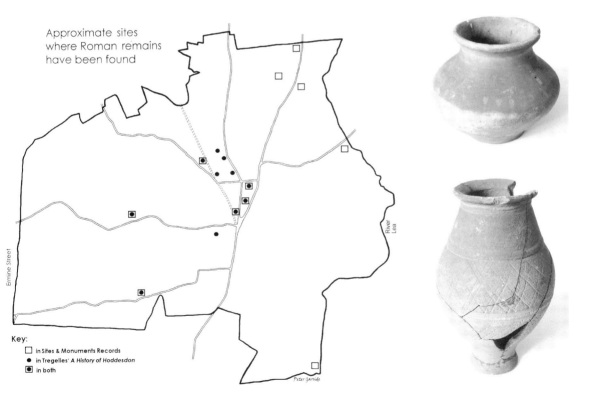

Approximate sites where Roman remains have been found

Ermine Street

River Lea

Key:
☐ in Sites & Monuments Records
● in Tregelles' *A History of Hoddesdon*
◉ in both

Peter Garside

7   Roman spearhead.
8   Samian ware shards found in gravel pits in Cock Lane.

was found in the same area. Burial urns and a Samian cup and jar rim were found in a gravel pit in the Westfield area. Early in the 20th century various fragments of pottery were retrieved from a gravel pit adjacent to Cock Lane. There were apparently a variety of types including fine red Samian ware, coarse Belgic everyday ware and also medieval pottery. A quern (hand mill) was found on the Hoddesdonbury estate and is thought to be either a Roman or a Saxon import.

On the whole the three hundred years of Roman rule in Hertfordshire was peaceful. The area was quite prosperous, but for the rural poor little had changed except the manner of their obligations. Under the Celtic tribal system they were beholden to a tribal leader who protected them in return for services or produce; under the Romans the relationship was that of landlord and tenant. The poorest tenants were, in effect, serfs tied to the land.

By AD 350 the Roman Empire was beginning to decline, and by the end of the century Roman troops were being withdrawn to defend other parts of the empire. The last of the troops went in AD 406 and the Roman province had disintegrated by the middle of the century.

Anglo-Saxon Rule

Saxons, Angles and Jutes were living in Britain before the end of Roman rule. They came as settlers and Roman army mercenaries. Once the Romans had left, more waves moved in, but there was no rapid take-over. The Romano-British held out in some areas until a decisive battle in about AD 570. There is some evidence that the triangle of land encompassed by St Albans, London and Colchester, with its fortified towns and strong Roman culture, was amongst the last areas to succumb to the Saxons.

The story of Anglo-Saxon take-over seems to have been one of infiltration over a long period, with gradual domination of a society that slowly disintegrated after the Romans had left. This disintegration may have been made worse by outbreaks of plague. The sophistication that the Romans had brought dwindled with their going: bartering replaced money transactions; wattle and skin buildings replaced brick and stone; subsistence farming replaced villa life. The changes must have affected town-dwellers and the higher echelons of society more than the rural community for whom agriculture was a continuing way of life.

Ermine Street continued to be used, although not kept in repair. The name is Saxon, derived from the personal name, Earn(a); it was Earninga stræt in the 900s and Ermingestrete by about 1090. The Roman crossing of the Lea at Ware fell into disrepair, and the easiest place to cross the Lea was now at Hertford: travellers from London left Ermine Street at what is now Hertford Heath and made their way north-west to the ford, stimulating the growing importance of Hertford in Saxon times. Although there may have been some residual Christianity from Roman times, the Angles and Saxons were pagan until conversion in the seventh century. The Synod of Hertford took place in AD 672 (although there is some dispute as to which Hertford was the venue) to establish the rules of government for the Roman Church, which had gained precedence over the Celtic Church at the earlier synod at Whitby.

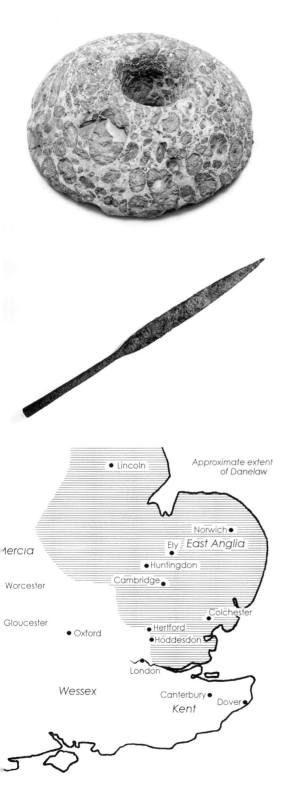

Few Saxon artefacts have been found in Hoddesdon. One reason for this may be that the simpler lifestyle of the Saxons meant that less durable items were being made. The quern mentioned above may have been Saxon and a Saxon spearhead was found near to the Roman remains when Roman Street was being built in the 19th century.

The kingdom of Mercia was the dominant power in all of mid-England from the seventh until the end of the eighth centuries. The Mercians had raided and traded their way to their dominant position, but feuding within the royal family opened the way for Wessex to become the predominant power early in the ninth century.

The Vikings (Danes) started to raid England in about AD 800. London was attacked in 839 with great loss of life and from then on the raiding became more persistent and the Danes began to settle. A 'Great Army' of Danes landed in 865 and within a few years only Wessex remained as a fully independent English kingdom. When Alfred, King of Wessex, defeated the Danish leader Guthrum in 886, the treaty they signed divided the country roughly on a diagonal from Chester to London. At the southern end, from Hertford to London, the boundary was the River Lea, so communities like Hoddesdon were, in effect, in border country. West of the Lea was English territory, east and north was Danelaw.

The peace brought about by the treaty only lasted a few years. Danish forces went out from their base in East Anglia, wreaking havoc, killing and plundering. In 894 a force of Danes from Mersea rowed up the Thames and the Lea and established a fort. This may have been anywhere from Hoddesdon to Hertford, but the most likely situation is Ware. In the summer of 895 a force of Londoners went up the Lea to confront the Danes but was beaten off. King Alfred arrived in the autumn to protect the

9 Upper part of a quern found in gravel pits in Cock Lane, 1880.

10 Saxon spearhead.

11 Map showing the extent of the Danelaw.

local people so that they could get their harvest in. Realising that he could trap the Danes, Alfred ordered forts to be built on either side of the river. Unable to get back down the Lea, the Danes abandoned their ships and got away overland.

Although this period had been costly for the English in terms of loss of men and cattle, the tide was turning and Danish occupation in this area probably only lasted for about one generation. Alfred's son, Edward, continued the struggle to regain English lands. In 913 he built two fortresses or burghs at Hertford and 'Hertfordshire' was created to support this base.

Early in the 11th century Anglo-Saxon and Danish areas combined under one ruler. On the death of Edward the Confessor, in 1066, the dispute as to whether he had nominated his Anglo-Saxon brother-in-law, Harold, or his Norman kinsman, William, as his successor was to have far-reaching consequences for everyone in the country.

II

The Norman Conquest and Beyond

✧

Before the Conquest

Domesday Book, written to provide William with details of his conquered land, also gives a picture of land ownership before the Conquest. The feudal system had operated in Anglo-Saxon England and remained the form of government used by William. He succeeded to all the Crown lands and rewarded his followers with grants of land, which they held as his tenants-in-chief.

Agriculture was based on the common field system as before. Manors would usually have three large arable fields and meads, all divided into strips. The fields were cultivated in rotation. The meads, otherwise called Lammas land, consisted of soil deposited from the streams on to the bog of the valley bottom and were used only for grazing. The marshes of the Lea valley were generally too wet even for rough grazing, until they were gradually drained and cleared of reeds and rushes. In Hoddesdon the names of some of the common fields have survived – Lowefeld, Westfeld, Middlefeld, Ditchfeld, Estfeld, Ryefeld, Lampitfeld, Southfeld – and are used today in street names.

Domesday Book has five entries for Hoddesdon, but this land was held by only three people before AD 1066. It is not possible to pinpoint the boundaries of their lands, but Tregelles, in

his *History of Hoddesdon*, deduced approximate locations based on some of the details in Domesday Book and later ownership of manors. Edeva the Fair, possibly synonymous with Edith Swannenhals who searched for Harold's body after the Battle of Hastings, held land in the south of Hoddesdon between Spital Brook and the Broxbournebury boundary. This land was an outlier (a piece of land detached from the manor) of the manor of Cheshunt. Godith, a vassal of Asgar, who was Harold's

12   Map showing principal pre-Conquest landowners.

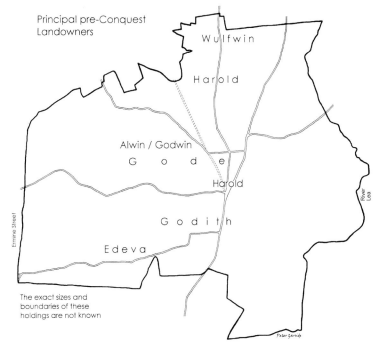

Principal pre-Conquest Landowners

Wulfwin

Harold

Alwin / Godwin

G o d e

Harold

Godith

Edeva

Ermine Street

River Lea

The exact sizes and boundaries of these holdings are not known

Peter Garside

Constable, held a strip of land between Spital Brook and what is now Lord Street, from west of Ermine Street to the Lea. Gode, a vassal of Queen Edith, held land between present-day Lord Street and Duke Street, extending along the line of the Hertford Road and including Dobbs Weir. Godith and Gode, despite being described as 'man of Asgar' and 'man of Queen Edith' respectively, were both women.

Gode's was the largest of the Hoddesdon holdings, amounting to 5¾ hides, the other two each being less than half of this. A 'hide' was a land measurement indicating the average agricultural holding of a peasant household or family unit, and as such could be a variable amount of actual land, but was often 120 acres. Other manors in the area were Hailey, which lay partly in the present Hoddesdon and was held by Wulfwin, and Rye, which was held by Swein. Both were vassals of King Harold. Wluueneuuiche may refer to an area in Hoddesdon around Woollens Brook; this was the land of Alwin and Godwin, vassals of Aelmer of Bennington. The area to the south of Hailey was part of Harold's manor of Great Amwell.

One area of Hoddesdon is recorded in the Domesday survey of Essex because it was an outlier of Harold's manor of Hatfield Broad Oak. This manor also held outliers in Hertford and Amwell. There is also a Domesday entry for 'Hodesdone' which was included in Chauncy's *The Historical Antiquities of Hertfordshire* as being Hoddesdon but, since it is in Braughing Hundred, it is thought to be a misspelling for Honesdone, an old version of Hunsdon.

Most of the Hoddesdon lands were held by people who were directly associated with Harold or his immediate circle. They must have been keenly aware of the danger as Harold's army marched north, probably passing close by along the old Roman road, to face the Danish threat at Stamford Bridge. Jubilation as the tired army returned triumphant to fight again at Hastings must have been followed by despair as news of the crushing defeat filtered through to them.

Aftermath

William led the Norman army north from Hastings in an arc around London, and 'ravaged all the parts he went over' according to the Anglo-Saxon Chronicle, until 'when the most harm was done', the English were forced to submit. The final surrender of the Anglo-Saxons took place three months after the invasion at Berkhamsted. It is generally thought that this was the Berkhamsted in the Tring valley, but it has been argued that the venue may have been Little Berkhamsted, which would have brought the pillaging army much closer to the local manors.

The value of the manors was certainly less after the Conquest than before, sometimes drastically so. Hailey and the Hoddesdon land of Godith each dropped to one eighth of their pre-Conquest value, and most of the other land went down to a half or a third of the 1066 value. The manor of Cheshunt including its Hoddesdon outlier was valued as a whole, and this sustained a loss of nearly a third. Recovery was slow and none of the manors had regained their 1066 values by the time of the Domesday survey in 1086.

Once William had secured his throne, his new English lands were divided among his Norman followers, many of whom held several parcels of land in different areas. Edeva's land was acquired by Alan, Count of Brittany. The manor of Hoddesdonbury was formed of this land. The mound which stands on the opposite side of Cock Lane to Hoddesdonbury House is thought to be a motte castle built in the early post-Conquest period. Earlier explanations of this mound were more in keeping with the (unsubstantiated) local legend that it was the burial place of a Dane named Oddo, after whom Hoddesdon was named. An archaeological dig in 1901 by Sir John Evans revealed a little pottery, a piece of a quern stone and some charred remains. Evans interpreted the site as a possible cremation site of a Danish chief and Tregelles favoured the idea of a Saxon or Danish stronghold.

The manor of Hoddesdonbury was held by the Bassingbourne family from the mid-13th century

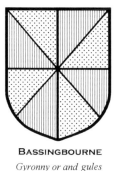
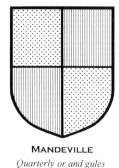

BASSINGBOURNE
Gyronny or and gules

MANDEVILLE
Quarterly or and gules

DE BOHUN
Azure a bend or cotised argent between six lions or

13   *Arms of Bassingbourne, Mandeville and de Bohun.*

until the mid-15th century. An incident in about 1400 illustrates the difficulties that could arise for an heir to a manor who was still a minor. Before Thomas Bassingbourne died, in the 1390s, he sold the wardship of his young son, John, for 100 marks to Alexander Besford (or Befford). Besford held both Hoddesdonbury and Bassingbourne for a while after Thomas Bassingbourne's death. The wardship was duly given to Besford by the owners-in-chief of Hoddesdonbury, the Archbishop of York and the Earl of Arundel. Besford then agreed to place the boy with Ralph Hamelyn and 'Ralph son of Richard' for 200 marks. However he later made a second grant of the wardship to Robert Whytington, John Befford, Richard Rehale and Thomas Throckmorton. They sent servants who collected the boy, but Ralph Hamelyn chased after them and took young John back by force. How the matter was resolved between the wards remains unknown, but John Bassingbourne did come into his inheritance in 1405.

Part of Godith's land went to Geoffrey de Mandeville, with Ralph de Limesi as tenant. The land remained in the Mandeville family until the late 12th century. From the early 13th century the de Bohuns became owners, and remained so until the last Humphrey de Bohun died in 1372, leaving no male heir. Two of his daughters, Eleanor and Mary, married into the Plantagenet family. In 1421 the manor went to the Crown as part of the Duchy of Lancaster, when it was claimed by Henry V as Mary's son and heir. For most of this period members of

the Bassingbourne family were tenants and lords of the manor, which became known as Bassingbourne manor. The manor house was probably sited at Hogges Hall.

The county histories mostly do not distinguish between the Hoddesdon manors. The *Victoria County History* includes both the Mandeville and the Brittany (later Earls of Richmond) allocations as the manor of Hoddesdonbury, but Tregelles in his *History of Hoddesdon* draws the distinctions given here.

Godith's other hide of land went to Count Eustace of Boulogne, and was held by the Canons of St Martins. The Canons still held the manor in 1290, when the Dean obtained an order to re-stock his park, Hoddesdon Park Wood, with two bucks and two does from the forest of Essex. There is a medieval moated site near the southern boundary of Hoddesdon Park Wood which is thought to be the location of the park keeper's lodge. The land was later disposed of to other manors and by 1355 Hoddesdon Park Wood was known as Bassingbourne's Park. The manor eventually merged with Langtons manor and was last mentioned in records in 1480.

Gode's land was divided between Edward the Sheriff (Edward of Salisbury) and Peter, a burgess, who was one of the king's thanes. Peter gave his land to the Abbey of Bermondsey in 1094, but subsequent ownership is unknown. The de Boxe family first appear in the records in 1198 as holders of land in Hoddesdon. Although Boxe manor is

14   *Hogges Hall, 1936. The shop-fronts are 20th-century. The house was renovated by J.A. Hunt in the 19th century, but has remains of its 15th-century hall.*

equated with Baas in two of the county histories, it seems more likely that the two are distinct manors. Baas manor was created when Broxbourne manor divided. In 1256 John de Bathonia (contracted to Baa) held nearly all the land of Broxbourne manor, except the manor house and desmesne lands which became the separate manor of Broxbournebury. In about 1250 Richard de Boxe held some of what had been Edward of Salisbury's land and the manor took his family name from this time, although there seem to have been Boxes in Hoddesdon some fifty years before that. By 1253 Richard de Boxe also held Hoddesdon manor which then ceased to exist as a separate entity.

Hoddesdon manor seems to have equated with the outlier of the manor of Hatfield Broad Oak. This outlier, along with the Amwell and Hertford outliers, was acquired by Ralph de Limesi, as was the manor of Amwell. The attachment of this area of Hoddesdon to Amwell resulted in this part of Hoddesdon being in the parish of Amwell until the 19th century. The manor was situated in the fork of the north-south road (where the Tower Centre now stands).

Peter de Valognes and Robert Gernon acquired the Wluueneuuiche land. The later manors of Sarmoners, Richard de Bury and Foxtons held land in this area. Wulfwin's manor of Hailey became the property of Geoffrey of Bec, but there was a dispute over some of the land. The Canons of Waltham claimed some of the Hailey woodland as did Ralph de Limesi, who held the lordship of Amwell among his possessions. He also asserted that three of the Hailey tenants who lived in the area of what is now the *Galley Hall* public house owed their feudal dues to Amwell and not Hailey. This claim was evidently upheld as these tenants later appear in manorial records as tenants of Amwell.

The Rye land went to the Bishop of Bayeux, with one Peter as his tenant. The marshy nature of the land is evident from the Domesday entry. No woodland is mentioned, but this small manor of half a hide was rated as having 200 eels from its weirs. In a record of 1261 it was referred to as the 'island of the Rye', an area of drier land among the marshes close to the junction of the River Lea and the River Stort.

Later manors

There were several small manors in the central part of Hoddesdon. Sarmoners existed from the middle of the 13th century. The last of the Sarmoners died in 1346 and the manor went to his heirs, one of whom was Richard de Bury. Boxe manor was acquired by the Langton family in the 14th century. Foxtons first appeared in the records in 1325, when it was the inheritance of Margery, the wife of Ralph de Foxton; by 1380 it was owned with Langtons.

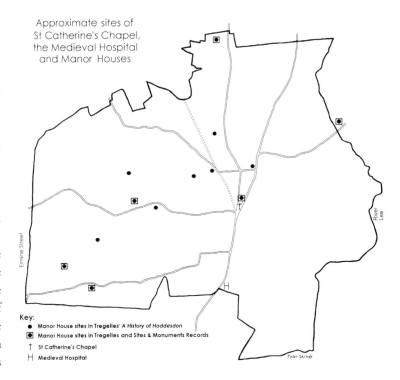

Approximate sites of
St Catherine's Chapel,
the Medieval Hospital
and Manor Houses

Key:
● Manor House sites in Tregelles' *A History of Hoddesdon*
◉ Manor House sites in Tregelles and Sites & Monuments Records
† St Catherine's Chapel
H Medieval Hospital

15   Map showing sites of manors.

There were Geddings in Hoddesdon from the 13th century, but the manor was not known by their name until the 14th century. The manor was probably formed of part of the outlier which had been conveyed to Ralph de Limesi after the Conquest. The land in this area was probably too marshy previously to be viable, but with the gradual drying out of the valley bottom it was possible to establish the manor there. In 1327 Edmund de Gedding got a grant of free warren from Edward III in his demesne land in Hoddesdon. Over the next fifty years the Geddings family acquired the smaller manors to the north of what is now Lord Street, and also owned land in Amwell and Thele. Soon after, the manor passed into other hands. John Chertsey, whose family had owned Baas manor in Broxbourne since 1297, acquired Geddings in 1383.

There seems to have been some dispute about the Langton acquisition of Boxes, because the manor was seized by the Crown in 1377. By 1392 John Sorel, bailiff of the Chertsey manors of Baas and Geddings, was also bailiff of Langtons, suggesting that the Chertseys had acquired this manor too. All three manors were in the possession of Thomas Gloucester by the 1430s. In 1448 they were acquired by William Say, with others, on behalf of his brother John.

III

Market Town

In England the feudal system broke down during the 13th and 14th centuries as the obligations and service due to superiors was commuted to monetary payments. The growth in population since the Norman Conquest had led to the need for more food and so to the growth of a more commercialised economy. Towns developed as the prospect of profit from the increasing volume of trade encouraged lords to apply for, and kings to grant, charters for markets and fairs; tradesmen and craftsmen were allowed to hold their properties by monetary rent, without the requirement of feudal service.

Gradual changes in road use resulted in Hoddesdon and the other Lea valley settlements being on the major road from London by the 13th century. The old Roman road, Ermine Street, to the west had deteriorated. The section south of Ware, built on London clay and having no readily available source of stone for repairs, had fallen into even more decay than other stretches. A bridge had been built at Ware some time before 1200, which drew traffic away from the crossing at Hertford. Despite sabotage of the bridge in 1191 and 1258 by citizens of Hertford, they were unable to win back their monopoly of the crossing of the Lea. The road through Broxbourne and Hoddesdon to Ware gradually became the accepted route, and Ermine Street became merely a drove road.

Hoddesdon was now at a parting of the ways. Travellers to Hertford could turn north-west here to take the road over Hertford Heath. Despite losing through-traffic and trade to Ware, Hertford remained a place of some importance because it was a royal borough whose castle was used by the monarchy until the 16th century. The road to Hertford branched off just north of Lord Street across an open area called Hoddesdon Green and was known as the Portway (market way) or 'Grene Street'. The road to the north branched in the centre of Hoddesdon, with one track leading to Hailey and the other to St Margarets and Great Amwell on the way to Ware. At first the latter route was used, but by 1374 the road via the end of Hailey Lane was the main road and the way through St Margarets was 'le Elde streete'. To the east, it was possible to cross to Essex at St Margarets, where there was a bridge by the 12th century, and at Rye House where there was a bridge and toll road by the middle of the 15th century.

In the middle of the 13th century Richard de Boxe owned land in the centre of Hoddesdon. He must have seen its potential, because in 1253 he obtained a royal grant from Henry III to hold a weekly Thursday market at his manor of Hoddesdon and also an annual fair lasting three days. A market cross was erected by 1256, but no further mention of the market appears in the records until 1468. The fair was to be held on the feast of St Martin on 11 November, and the days preceding and following. A later owner, Henry Bourchier, Earl of Essex, petitioned for a change in the date of the fair during the reign of Henry VIII. It was altered to the feast of St Martin in summer, on 4 July, and the days preceding and following. A further charter issued by Elizabeth I concerning the market and fair granted

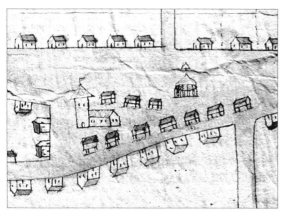

16 Detail from map c.1570, showing the market cross, market stalls and chapel. © The Marquess of Salisbury

the holding of two fairs, reverting to the November St Martin's day and adding 29 June, St Peter's day. The November fair lapsed, but the June fair was a toy fair in the late 18th century and was held as a pleasure fair well into the 20th century.

The first mention of a chapel in Hoddesdon is in 1242, when a claim was made against Humphrey de Bassingbourne and his mother, Albreda, in respect of the chapel. The Bassingbournes held Hoddesdonbury manor and were tenants of the de Bohuns in Bassingbourne manor, which implies that the chapel was situated on one of these properties, both of which lay in the parish of Broxbourne. No further mention of the chapel appears, but Tregelles quotes a case brought against a Hoddesdon priest, Roger the clerk, who was accused of robbery and assault in 1313. Roger's co-accused was his *daughter*. If Roger was in fact a priest, he had ignored his church's law of celibacy, in addition to his other faults.

In 1336 William de la Marche, a parishioner of Amwell, obtained permission from the king to build 'anew' a chapel in honour of St Katherine on land he owned in Hoddesdon. The chapel may have been for William's private use, since the parish church was about two miles away, but may also have provided a place of worship for pilgrims travelling from London to Walsingham. As a pilgrim venue, the Shrine of Our Lady at Walsingham, established early in the 12th century, was second in popularity only to the

shrine of St Thomas à Becket at Canterbury. It attracted many foreign as well as British travellers, who would appreciate an overnight stopping place which could also cater for their spiritual needs.

William is said to have lived just to the north of the site of the chapel, at a building later known as the Maidenhead. He was described in the court rolls as 'clericus', but may well have been the William de la Marche who appears in charters of the time holding the office of King's Cook. An enquiry conducted by the lord of Amwell in 1364 concluded that this chapel was entirely within the parish of Amwell: the boundary between the two parishes was marked by stakes 40 feet from the chapel. An Amwell man, Richard atte Pond, had also planted a tree six feet within these marks so that the parishioners of Amwell could be sure they were within their own parish. It goes on to state that one 'Gilbert Messanger within the same marks … was left half deade' by the parishioners of Broxbourne, implying a rather violent rivalry between the two parishes! The northern boundary of the parish of Broxbourne, taking in most of Hoddesdon, was described in 1397 in a settlement of a dispute which arose about tithes of hay and corn grown in certain fields, and no specific reference to the position of the chapel was mentioned. The parochial status of the chapel was disputed again in the 17th century and the 1839 tithe award shows it in the parish of Broxbourne.

One of the priests of the chapel, Peter Meedwyn, or Needwyn, who died in 1465, was commemorated in the earliest known brass (now lost) in St Augustine's Church, Broxbourne. The inscription recorded that he was chaplain of Hoddesdon chapel and he is not listed as a vicar of Broxbourne or Great Amwell, so it seems that the chapel had its own priest at this period.

In the 1530s the incumbent was a man called Lee. This priest was involved in a case reported in the Court of the Star Chamber Proceedings of Henry VIII. (The Star Chamber in the Palace of Westminster, so-called from its star-bedecked ceiling, was where the Privy Council met. At this time, one of its functions was to deal with serious misdemeanours such as riots.) The report to the court gives only the complainants' version of events, and so may well be biased, but it shows how a minor incident could escalate into a violent confrontation. Tregelles, in his *History of Hoddesdon*, quoted the report in full.

In August 1534 two ladies were travelling north to Northamptonshire with a group of servants and others to prepare for the funeral of Sir William Fitzwilliam, whose body was to be brought from London the next day. Just south of Hoddesdon they came up to a local butcher, Robert Mitchell (spelt Mychell in the petition), who was accompanied by a boy on a horse loaded with sheepskins. One of the servants 'gentely desyered' Mitchell and his boy to move aside, to ensure that the ladies' horses would not shy away from the pungent sheepskins and so that they would not have to pass through the dust created by Mitchell's horses. (If the manner in which the travellers expressed their desires was not as gentle as they claimed, that might explain the following events; a case of 16th-century road rage, perhaps.) Mitchell replied that he had as much right to use the road as them, and when asked again he lost his temper. He would not be pacified and, refusing to go ahead or drop behind, he insisted on riding alongside them into Hoddesdon.

Once there, he turned and threatened them with a club. His swearing and threats brought people out on to the street. Apparently 200 men and women armed with all manner of weapons started laying into the travellers, and carried off three of their servants to the cage (the local lock-up). The remnants of the party repaired to an inn, where they were pelted with dirt and stones, and had ale thrown in their faces. Mitchell made it known to them that he was the constable of the town, and would have arrested them as well, had it not been for the intercession of a local man (unnamed).

The following day, the funeral cortege of Sir William Fytzwilliam set out. This party was also accosted in Hoddesdon, not by Robert Mitchell this time, but by Lee, the priest. Lee stopped one of the mourners and demanded the right to bury the corpse. As he seemed determined to cause trouble, they bargained with him, and Lee eventually accepted a payment of 20d. to allow the cortege to continue. Tregelles' researches did not bring any subsequent legal action to light, beyond the presentation of a bill of costs at Hertford Quarter Sessions.

Lee was the last priest of the chapel, after which time it was served from Amwell. After the dissolution of the monasteries in 1536 the flow of pilgrims ceased. The chapel was used on occasion by the vicars of both Broxbourne and Amwell to preach sermons and hold services. It also served a number of secular purposes: as a schoolroom, a venue for the manor court, and a place to conduct business deals.

There are not many local records around the time of the Black Death outbreak of 1348, but names of under-age heirs in the manorial court records of 1349 may indicate that the disease took its toll in Hoddesdon. Another much feared disease was leprosy, although this ceased to be endemic in England by 1500. There was a reference to leprosy in Hoddesdon in 1382, when the St Martins manor court 'presented Eva Crumpton as a leper living in the house of Richard Auncel to the great injury of his neighbours'. Richard was ordered to remove her under a penalty of 20s.

Hoddesdon had a hospital which was mentioned in the records of the Diocese of Ely in 1390, when the bishop granted indulgences for the poor and lepers of that house. In 1394 a tenant of Hoddesdonbury called William of the Hospital may have been master there. It seems likely that this early hospital was identical with the almshouse for the poor of the 16th century situated near Spital Brook, described as having been founded for 'poor Lasars Leperous and Impotent persons'. The case has been put that the almshouse was a later foundation, perhaps late 15th-century; and that the leper hospital may have been sited elsewhere, based on the argument that a leper hospital would not have been close to the highway. However, other such hospitals were built on thoroughfares. Also, the Spitalbrook site had the

17   Seal of Hoddesdon's medieval hospital. By permission of the British Library, Gray Birch Catalogue of Seals, 3285 (DC G 19).

characteristics usually required for leper hospitals, in that it was close to a running stream and was close to but separate from an urban centre, about equidistant from both Hoddesdon and Broxbourne.

As the number of cases of leprosy fell most of the leper hospitals changed their primary use, and this seems to be so for Hoddesdon's hospital. Although it is still described as the 'Lazar House' in a bequest in the will of Sir William Say in 1529, it was probably already simply a hospital or almshouse, and by the time of an enquiry in 1568 it was described as 'the poore house or hospitell' for the poor and sick with no reference to any specific illness. It may be that it survived beyond the time of the dissolution of the monasteries, the only medieval Hertfordshire hospital to do so, because it became a purely secular almshouse.

Two seals in the British Library have been attributed to Hoddesdon's hospital. Both are 15th-century, one showing St Laud and St Anthony and the other St Clement and St Laud, so there may have been a change in dedication.

The poor of Hoddesdon were also catered for in almshouses given by Richard Rich, a local landowner, in 1440. They stood on the east side of the High Street a little to the north of Lords Lane. Their position was such that there was some dispute in the

17th century as to whether they stood in Great Amwell parish or in Broxbourne parish. The almshouses were not the only charitable gift of Richard Rich. In his will of 1463 he left £10 to be distributed among the poor of Hoddesdon, 4d. a week to each of the almshouse inmates to pray for his soul, and 20 marks towards the marriage portions of poor but honest girls. His interests extended to the fabric of the town because he bequeathed the cost of gravelling the street from north to south. Richard Rich owned land and buildings in Hoddesdon including two inns, the *George* and the *Cock*, and the dwelling house known as the Falcon or the Falcon on the Hoop.

The Peasants' Revolt of the 14th century did not seriously affect eastern Hertfordshire. Essex, one of the centres of rebellion, was isolated from Hertfordshire because of the marshy nature of the Lea valley. News of the deeds of the Kentish and Essex rebels in London spread north via Barnet. The revolt was centred mainly on disputes between the Abbot of St Albans and his tenants, and disturbances occurred in towns in the west of Hertfordshire. A murder at Waltham Cross and a robbery at Cheshunt were linked to the rebellion, but Hoddesdon appears to have remained quiet.

Rye House and the Ogard Family

Andrew Ogard bought the manors of Hailey and Thele (known jointly as Goldingtons as the result of more than a century of owners of that name) in 1423 and acquired the manor of Rye in 1443. A Dane, originally called Andre Pedersen, he was born about 1400. He became a soldier in the English army during the period of great successes under Henry V, and much of his wealth probably came from plunder in the wake of these victories, an acceptable form of income at the time. From land and castles in France it was estimated that he derived an income of £1,000 a year, as well as possessing 7,000 marks worth of French gold.

Ogard served with the Duke of Bedford and was knighted after the English victory at Verneuil in

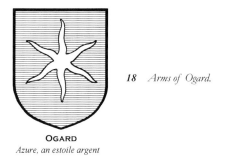

18   Arms of Ogard.

OGARD
Azure, an estoile argent

1424. He continued in the duke's service as a chamberlain and councillor, becoming a naturalised Englishman in the 1430s. When the Duke of Bedford died in 1435 Ogard joined the Duke of York, whose retinue included a number of successful veteran soldiers. York formed an alliance with the Duke of Gloucester, whose policies opposed those of the Duke of Suffolk, uncle and councillor of Henry VI. National politics does not seem, in this case, to have affected dealings between neighbours. When John Say, at that time a staunch supporter of the Duke of Suffolk, acquired the manors of Baas, Langtons, Foxtons and Geddings in 1448, Ogard acted as one of the trustees.

In addition to Rye, Hailey and Thele, Andrew Ogard held the manor of Newgates (the site of which is marked by Newgate Wood to the north-east of Stanstead Abbotts), and also had 'free warren' (the right to hunt small game) in Thele, Hoddesdon, Ware, Widford, Hunsdon, Eastwick and Stanstead Abbotts. The granting of free warren in areas beyond his manors was apparently unusual. Salmon, in his *History of Hertfordshire*, suggested that the giving of these privileges to Ogard was a reminder to lords who may have retained Yorkist sympathies to mend their ways. However, Ogard was himself a supporter of the Duke of York; and there is insufficient information about some of the local lords affected to judge their national allegiances.

Ogard obtained a licence from Henry VI to empark his manor of Rye and to build a house there with turrets, battlements and machicolations. Rye House was one of the earliest brick-built houses in the county. Its defences were designed to ward off minor incursions. Fifteenth-century England could be a lawless place, and there were instances of seizures of manor houses by covetous rivals, but the large oriel windows and elaborate brickwork of the gatehouse show that it was primarily an impressive domestic building, not a military stronghold. William Worcestre's *Itineraries*, a record of his travels in the late 15th century, gives some details of Rye House, which he visited in 1478. As well as dimensions of the buildings and courtyards, he stated that the manor had cost £1,100. Other costs are not so clear from the text, but have been interpreted as follows: the granary, 16 horses, 30 cows, and the storehouse of goods, 2,200 marks; and building the inner court with brick, and the rooms with the cloister, including repairs, more than 2,000 marks. Worcestre also wrote that Andrew Ogard maintained a chapel in the house, with priests, clerks and choristers, at a cost of £100 a year. All that now remains of Rye House is the gatehouse.

19   Rye House gatehouse.

As lord of the manor, Ogard was responsible for maintaining the bridge over the river and keeping a causeway across the meadows. Travellers paid a charge for using this road, which was a convenient route to Suffolk and Norfolk, via Bishops Stortford. It remains a toll road to this day.

Through his wife, Alice, he acquired Buckenham castle and manor in Norfolk; and he was patron of Wymondham Priory, being responsible for its conversion into an independent abbey.

Andrew Ogard died in 1454, leaving a son, Henry, who was then only four. Wardship of Henry was granted to the Bishop of Durham in 1461 and transferred to the Duke of Clarence, when Henry was married in 1463, at the age of thirteen. The manor of Rye was held by the Ogard family until 1560.

The Say Family

John Say

From the middle of the 15th century, many of the manors in Hoddesdon and Broxbourne were acquired by the Say family. John Say's lineage is uncertain. He and his brother, William, seem to have adopted the name of Say. His family name may have been Heron (or Heroun) or Fiennes: if Heron, then his connection to the Say family was not a blood tie, but the name was used by one of his forebears who acquired it by right of a wife of a previous marriage; if Fiennes, then he was probably descended through the female line from Geoffrey de Say, as was James Fiennes, Lord Say and Sele, with whom he seems to have been closely connected.

Well connected, probably well educated and evidently ambitious, John Say became a member of the royal household, and held the posts of King's Sergeant and Yeoman of the Chamber. In 1444 he was appointed Coroner of the Marshalsea, for which he received a grant of £10 a year, and in 1445 he became Keeper of the Privy Palace of Westminster with an allowance of 6d. a day. He had married Elizabeth, daughter of Lawrence Cheney of Cambridgeshire in about 1440, and through his father-in-law's influence he became parliamentary represent-

20 *Drawing of the brass on the tomb of John and Elizabeth Say, from* History of Hertfordshire, *J.E. Cussans, vol.2, p.184 (Hertford), 1874-1878.*

ative for Cambridgeshire in 1447 and again in 1449, when he was Speaker.

Say was a supporter of the Duke of Suffolk, uncle and councillor of Henry VI. The Duke of Suffolk's policies led to loss of land in France and growing lawlessness at home; he and his circle, Say included, were also accused of lining their own pockets at the Crown's expense. In 1450 Suffolk was indicted by Parliament and banished by Henry VI, but on his way to exile in France was waylaid and killed. The matter did not rest there. Jack Cade of Kent led a rebellion demanding social and political reforms including the removal from office of Suffolk's clique. The rebels succeeded in taking London for a few days and indicted several of Suffolk's supporters with treason. Some, including John Say, were later acquitted, but James Fiennes, Lord Say and Sele, and his son-in-law, William Crowmer, Sheriff of Kent, were executed before the rebels were dispersed.

In 1451 John Say's name appeared on a list of people whom the Commons recommended should be removed from the king's presence for life. This does not seem to have had an adverse effect on his parliamentary career, because he was a Member of Parliament again in 1453, this time for Hertfordshire. He represented the county in the parliaments of the 1450s and '60s, being Speaker of the House in 1463-5 and 1467-8. He did, however, change his allegiance from Lancastrian to Yorkist in the early 1450s. When Henry VI had his first bout of mental illness in 1453, the Duke of York became Protector and a new Privy Council was assembled in which 15 Lancastrians were expelled and five Yorkists were appointed, one of whom was John Say. When the king recovered in 1455 and the Duke of York was dismissed, the stage was set for battle between the two factions. The Yorkists triumphed and the Duke of York's son became Edward IV in 1461. Although John Say had been described as an 'Esquier of ye body' to Henry VI in 1455, he was considered to be a sound enough Yorkist to be knighted by Edward in 1465. In 1469 he was appointed to a commission enquiring into abuses of the Royal Mint, but after that seems to have concerned himself more with local matters.

John Say acquired the manors of Baas, Langtons, Foxtons, Geddings, Mareons, Halles and Perers (Baas, Mareons or Marions and Halles are in Broxbourne; Perers is in Cheshunt) in 1448, perhaps financed by profits accrued while he was a member of Suffolk's circle. His older brother, William, and others including his father-in-law and Andrew Ogard of Rye House acted as trustees for him. The group of manors bought by Say appears to have been held jointly from that time; the manor house at Baas was the dwelling house when the Says were in residence, but they also had a house in London.

John and Elizabeth Say had five sons, two of whom apparently died young, and four daughters. Two of Elizabeth's descendants became Henry VIII's

wives: her great-granddaughter by her first marriage was Anne Boleyn and one of John and Elizabeth's great-granddaughters was Jane Seymour. Their daughter, Katherine, married Thomas, son of John Bassingbourne of Hoddesdonbury. Katherine and Thomas lived mainly at Woodhall, which had been held jointly with Astwick by the Bassingbourne family since 1198. By 1467 John Say was leasing Hoddesdonbury, and it was bought by his son, William, from Katherine and Thomas in 1493 or '94, although Katherine retained an interest. After Thomas's death she relinquished the manor to William.

John Say owned other properties in Hertfordshire, including Weston, purchased in 1452, and Bedwell and Little Berkhamsted, purchased in 1466. He acquired the manor of Sawbridgeworth in 1468 on the death of John Heron, who had died without issue.

Say's political machinations probably had little impact on the tenants of his manors. Of more importance to them would have been that the manors were well run, as is indicated by records such as manor court rolls and bailiffs' accounts of his Hoddesdon and Broxbourne lands. He was appointed to a commission of 1476 charged with the repair of the banks of the River Lea. In 1468 he obtained an inspeximus (a charter in which an earlier charter is inspected and confirmed) of Richard de Boxe's grant for the annual fair and weekly market, which, although primarily of benefit to himself as holder of the market rights, must also have been of benefit to the people of the town.

The market rights originally granted to Richard de Boxe by Henry III had descended to Langtons manor when it took over Boxes, and hence came to John Say when he acquired Langtons with his other manors in 1448. Confirmation of the grant was important because in 1441 Henry VI had granted to Hertford the right to hold a weekly market to the exclusion of any others within seven miles. Hoddesdon's original market charter had ended with the words 'unless that fair and market be to the annoyance of neighbouring markets and fairs'. The bailiffs

Say Family Tree

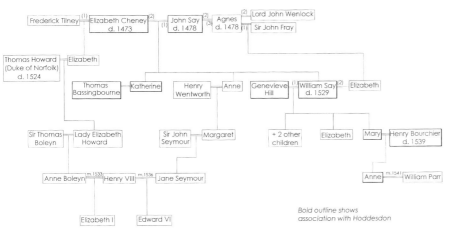

21   Tomb of John and Elizabeth Say, St Augustine's church, Broxbourne.

Bold outline shows association with Hoddesdon

of Hertford complained that the Hoddesdon market did indeed annoy them and although John Say obtained his confirmation from Edward IV, the dispute between the two towns lasted until the reign of Elizabeth nearly a hundred years later. A new market cross was erected in Hoddesdon at about this time, probably to celebrate the town's successful bid and to advertise its status.

Elizabeth Say died in 1473. John Say married his second wife, Agnes, in 1477. She had been married twice before; firstly to Sir John Fray, who died in 1461, and secondly to John Lord Wenlock, killed at the battle of Tewkesbury in 1471. Sir John Fray served on many government commissions, and was involved in property transfers and the wardship of heirs during their minority, which could be a very lucrative business. He was a considerable landowner, but his only involvement in the manors of Hoddesdon was that he held Hoddesdonbury for a period in the 1450s in return for money lent to John Bassingbourne. John Say died in 1478 and Agnes died only a few months later.

Sir John and Dame Elizabeth Say are buried in an altar tomb in St Augustine's church in Broxbourne. On the marble slab on top of the tomb are enamelled brasses of John (without the head) and Elizabeth. The main fabric of the church is 15th-century; and although there seems to be no documentary evidence,

apart from the building of the south chapel by Robert Stowell for him in 1476, the suggestion that Sir John was the founder, perhaps rebuilding or extending a previous structure, seems quite plausible. The manors of the parish had previously mostly been held by different owners, but Sir John had a considerable interest in the area as holder of a large proportion of the manors; and he had the fortune with which to fund such an undertaking.

William Say

William was the eldest son of Sir John and Elizabeth Say, and he inherited the Broxbourne and Hoddesdon manors on his father's death in 1478. He bought

Hoddesdonbury, which his father had been leasing, in 1493. To these he added Weston Argentein, Bennington and Tolmers. He served on local commissions and was Sheriff of Hertfordshire in 1483-4.

He was knighted by Richard III in 1483, but unlike his father he seems not to have taken much part in national politics, and the only other instance of his attracting royal notice was on the occasion of a dispute with a neighbour, Sir John Fortescue of Ponsbourne, in about 1500. Both men apparently intended to go to the Hertford Sessions with their followers to try to force the issue. However, news of the affair reached Henry VII, and Sir William received a letter signed by the king ordering him not to take action. Fortescue received a similar letter and the situation seems to have been defused.

Sir William Say was married to Genevieve, née Hill, and they had two sons who both died young, and two daughters, Elizabeth and Mary. After Genevieve's death he married Elizabeth, daughter of Sir John Fray. (Fray had been his stepmother's first husband.) In 1522 Sir William added the north chapel to the church of St Augustine, Broxbourne, and he also gave gifts of plate and vestments to the church. He died in 1529 and is buried in a tomb surmounted by a canopy with octagonal pillars under the arch opening into his chapel.

In his will he left money to various charitable and religious establishments so that prayers might be said for his soul. Among the recipients were the poor of Broxbourne and certain other parishes, religious orders, the lasar house at Hoddesdon (6s. 8d.) and every lasar house within 20 miles of London (20d.). He was concerned, too, about the state of the roads. There was a specific bequest to be used in 'amendynge of fowlle and noyous highe wayes in Hertfordshyre where most nede is', and these 'fowlle and noyous highe wayes' were mentioned again in a bequest in which the proceeds of a sale of lands were to be distributed to the poor, used to improve the roads, provide marriages for poor maidens and other charitable deeds as deemed best by his executors for 'the wealle of my sowlle'.

22   Tomb of William Say, St Augustine's church, Broxbourne.

The manors descended to the younger daughter, Mary, and her husband Henry Bourchier. Their daughter, Anne, inherited in 1539, when her father died after a fall from a horse. Anne married Sir William Parr in 1541. He was the brother of Catherine Parr, the last wife of Henry VIII. The manors were apparently settled on Anne by an Act of 1543/4, but in 1547 Parr rejected her and obtained a special Act in 1548 to declare her children bastards. After the death of Edward VI, Parr supported the bid for the throne of Lady Jane Grey, and was attainted in 1553 when Mary triumphed. He lost his estates, including those settled on Anne. Queen Mary granted Baas to the Earl of Arundel and others, but allowed Anne use of it; and when Elizabeth I came to the throne, Anne was granted life interest in Hoddesdonbury and Perers, and perhaps the other manors too. There was a family connection between Elizabeth I and Anne through Elizabeth Cheney, wife first of Frederick Tilney, then of John Say, which perhaps prompted the queen's act of generosity.

Queen Elizabeth granted Hoddesdonbury and Perers to Robert Earl of Leicester in 1566, who soon conveyed them to Sir William Cecil. In 1569 Elizabeth granted Baas to Sir William, who bought out Anne's interest in the manors to become absolute owner.

IV

Elizabethan Hoddesdon

Sir William Cecil (created Lord Burghley in 1571), Secretary of State and later Lord High Treasurer to Elizabeth I, had started building his house at Theobalds in Cheshunt in 1554, and held other land in the area. Despite all the other calls on his time, he took great interest in his Broxbourne and Hoddesdon manors, and in *c.*1570 commissioned a map to be drawn by Israel Amyce of Cheshunt.

Hoddesdonbury had been let in 1541 to Thomas Thorowgood, and the manor house and woods continued to be let to members of the Thorowgood family and others until 1614. Thomas Thorowgood made profitable use of his land by subletting it in smaller parcels. He also acquired Geddings manor house and was in possession of the house called the Falcon (or Fawkon) on the Hoop (or Ring) in 1539. This building, despite its name, does not seem ever to have been an inn. A later building on the site was an inn, the *Griffin*, for a short while. The shopping precinct of Fawkon Walk was named from the Fawkon on the Hoop. The Thorowgood family also owned property between the Fawkon and Lord's Lane (Lord Street) to the north. Thomas took arms in 1573, elevating his status from 'yeoman' to 'gentleman'. He died in February 1576/7, and his wife Agnes in 1577.

Their son, William, a London draper, inherited most of the Hoddesdon property, including the Fawkon on the Hoop. He bought the *Cock Inn* in 1591. It stood on the corner of the High Road and Cock Lane, on the site later to house the Grange. A wealthy man, William left charitable bequests to Hoddesdon and Broxbourne when he died in 1602.

23   *William Cecil, Lord Burghley. Library Illustrations Collection (HALS)*

Thomas, William's eldest son, inherited his London property; the family of John, the second son who pre-deceased William, inherited the Hoddesdon property; and Richard, the third son, seems to have carried on the drapery business. Thomas had one daughter, Elizabeth.

The Thorowgood family were widespread locally. There were branches in Great Amwell, Ware and Brickendon. John Thorowgood of Amwell, a cousin of William, leased the Hoddesdon woods from Lord Burghley in 1595. Woodland management at this

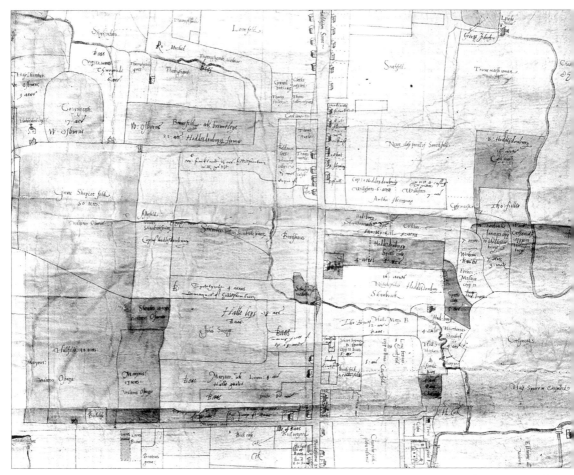

24   *Detail from map c.1570, showing Hoddesdon from the middle of the town in the north to Broxbourne church in the south and from Hoddesdonbury in the west to the Lynch mill and stream in the east. © The Marquess of Salisbury*

time consisted of coppicing the underwood (in this case on a ten-year cycle) and allowing a few trees to grow on to maturity for timber. The products of coppicing were roundwood or tallwood (coppiced poles) and faggots (the side branches and small pieces made into bundles). With his partner, William Keeling of London, he set about marketing the wood products differently than of old, which caused much resentment among the people of Hoddesdon. Previously, they had paid for the underwood by the acre, and the felling and sorting into roundwood and faggots were left to them. Thorowgood and Keeling decided to do these jobs themselves and sell the finished products.

A petition was sent to Lord Burghley complaining of labourers losing their jobs and exorbitant prices being charged for the wood. Keeling and Thorowgood countered by claiming that the principal petitioners had acquired signatures by threats, by persuading people to sign or to allow their names to be used without knowing the content of the petition, by signing up people who were not inhabitants of the town, and even by duplicating some of the names. Answering the complaints Keeling and Thorowgood asserted that the labourers would not accept a fair rate for the work, and that the prices asked were as cheap as any in the surrounding area.

25 Arms of Thorowgood, from the Thorowgood manuscript book, compiled by Robert Thorowgood in 1724. HALS D/EHx/F110
26 Page from the Thorowgood manuscript book. HALS D/EHx/ F110

A further petition by the townspeople stressed their poverty, claimed that Keeling and Thorowgood had a monopoly on the available wood, that the faggots and bundles of roundwood would be under-sized, and that the poorest people would be priced out of the market altogether. Keeling and Thorowgood went on the offensive in their reply, which incidentally gives an insight into the make-up of the town at that time. They estimated that the town had 130 'aunceant' (ancient) tenements. The inhabitants, they claimed, far from being poor, had made their outhouses into houses and erected new cottages for incomers, and that some of these encroached on Lord Burghley's land. They went on to say that 30 of the 130 were worth at least £100; another 30 were innkeepers making a good living, but using excessive firewood because they brewed their own beer and kept blazing fires going; 20 either had their own woods, or were not tenants of Lord Burghley and so not eligible to get their wood from him; and 15 were tradesmen making a good living. For the remainder they put forward an aid scheme. John's cousin, William, would keep a store of faggots which would be sold to the poor at 1d. a faggot. The Thorowgood and Keeling method of marketing would, they claimed, benefit the slightly better off who would be able to buy a load of the prepared wood whereas they would not have been able to afford to bid for an area of woodland. They also offered access to the woods for the poor so that they might glean any remaining dead wood when the re-growth after cutting had been enclosed, as long as a guarantor was willing to assure that no damage to hedges or growing wood would be done.

However, the dispute continued, probably because there had been advantages to the buyers in the old method. They had been able to take as much of the underwood as they could cut without regard to damage to the woodland because they had no responsibility for ensuring regeneration. Lack of supervision meant that the timber trees, which were not included in the deal, might occasionally be felled without their loss being noticed. However, it seems

27   Drawing of the brass of John Borrell, St Augustine's church. The brass is incomplete; the lower part of the legs and the feet are missing.

that Thorowgood and Keeling were successful in the long run as the leasing of the woods for a period of years subsequently became an accepted practice.

Several of Hoddesdon's inns date from the 16th century. Of the 30 innkeepers complained of by Thorowgood and Keeling in their answer to the townspeople's petition, 29 are listed. Of these, five are denoted by the inn's sign rather than the proprietor's name: the *Lyon*, the *Swanne*, the *Bell*, the *Chekquers* and the *George*.

The *Lyon*, called the *Star* before 1530, was owned by John Borrell, Sergeant-at-Arms to Henry VIII. Borrell also owned properties on the site later occupied by Yew House. He died in 1531. The inn had become the *Black Lion* ('the *Blake Lyon*') by 1554, and in 1568 the '*Starre* alias the *Lyon*' was bought by William Frankland. Frankland's heirs sold the inn to Lord Burghley in 1580. In the 1590s Hercules Wytham, tenant of the *Black Lion*, was asking Lord

28   *The* Salisbury Arms *inn.*
29   *The* White Swan *inn.*
30   *The* Bell *inn.*

31 *The* Bull *inn, c.1960.*

Burghley for money for repair of the inn, and claiming that its poor state had resulted in the *Chequers* obtaining all the wine licences. The *Black Lion* was renamed the *Salisbury Arms* in the 19th century. The inn had a bowling green, mentioned by the Reverend Thomas Hassall of Amwell in his account of walking his parish bounds in 1634-5, and shown on a plan of the inn of 1692.

The *Swan* or *White Swan* was built in the late 16th century. It was owned by the Sharnbrookes, a prosperous family who held property in Hoddesdon and Hailey. About 1600, the *White Swan* was acquired by John Bayley, who married into the Sharnbrooke family.

The *Bell* referred to in Thorowgood and Keeling's statement was later called the *Bull*. It was an inn by 1575. The name had changed to the *Bull* by about 1720 when it was mentioned in verses by Matthew Prior, and had presumably changed before 1660 when the current *Bell* took that name. The *Bell*,

formerly the *Holly Bush* and then the *Blue Bell*, is basically a 16th-century house. It was a private residence known as Conysby's in 1546, when it was owned by John Conysby, rector of Amwell. Called Cunnisbyes by Thomas Hassall, it belonged to Gamaliel Hales in the early 1600s and to Thomas Johnson in 1634. It became an inn about 1660 and was re-leased by Thomas Johnson and others to Arthur Windus.

The *Chequers* stood on the site now occupied by Pearces the Bakers (87 High Street). It was first mentioned in a rental in 1467 and remained as an inn until the 18th century. An inn called the *George* or the *St George* was situated opposite the end of Conduit Lane. It was recorded before 1464 when it was held by Richard Rich, and remained in the possession of the family until 1528. It was mentioned in the Victuallers Billetting Returns of 1756 and in local directories in 1826 and 1839, but was

demolished in 1846. An inn at Spitalbrook, licensed from 1866, took the
name of the *George*.

The *Golden Lion*, another long-
established inn, stands on the site of
a house known as the White Hinde
before 1535. At that time it may well
not have been an inn, but seems to
have been one in 1591 although it was
mentioned in the records because it
did not have a licence. By 1600 it
belonged to Thomas Thorowgood,
probably as a dwelling house, or possibly an alehouse, rather than an inn,
because it was described as a
'messuage' rather than a 'hospicum',

32   The Golden Lion *inn.*

which was the word used for the *Black Lion*. It passed
from Thomas Thorowgood to his daughter, Elizabeth, and then to her grandson Marmaduke Rawdon
in 1667. It was still known as the *White Hinde* at this
date, but was the *Golden Lion* by 1756.

The *Maidenhead* was an inn by 1576, when it was
held by Thomas Thorowgood. There had been a
house on the site since the 14th century, when it had
been owned by William de la Marche, but it may be

that it became an inn during Elizabeth's reign, given
its name with reference to the Virgin Queen. The
building on the corner of Yewlands was probably an
inn in 1575, when it was owned by the Tebbes family.
It was known then as *Lez Harteshorne*, but became
the *Five Bells* in 1680. It subsequently became a private
house called South End, and is now known as Harteshorne. North of Cock Lane, where the Grange now
stands, was an inn called the *Cock*, which was built
before 1500. The inn was bought by
William Thorowgood in 1591 and descended to Elizabeth Thorowgood on
her marriage in 1611 to Marmaduke
Rawdon. Next to this inn was a
property called Thurgoods and next
again another inn originally called the
Birdbolt. It changed its name in 1600
to the *Crown*.

Most inns and some private houses
had been accustomed to brew their own
beer, but some beer was bought from
brewers. In 1589 William Thorowgood
applied unsuccessfully to build a brewery on a piece of land called Hallmores,
which lay just to the east of the road at
Spitalbrook. He claimed it would be
of great benefit to the people of

33   The Maidenhead *inn, 1872.*

Hoddesdon, who 'to their great charge and trouble are enforced to be served from Brewers farre of by reason there is not any Brewhouse in the Towne'.

The old hospital building near Spital Brook was leased by William Smith in 1624, and he applied for a licence for an alehouse there in 1636. The present building on the site stands a little further south than its predecessor and dates from 1806. This was the new *George*, licensed in 1866. But before it became an alehouse the old hospital was to have another use. It was situated within the manor of Hoddesdon-bury and was leased, in 1561, by Lady Anne Bourchier to William Smythe. Smythe sold the lease on to Robert Reeve, who sub-let the hospital and the guardianship of the inmates to Thomas Jackson for 60s. a year. It seems that the hospital had capacity for 12 men and women, but there were eight plus Jackson and his wife in 1568. During Jackson's tenure, Sir William Cecil became owner of the manor, and it was to him that Jackson appealed in 1568. His complaint was that although Reeve had agreed to keep the hospital in repair he had not done so. He claimed that two groves, Spittle Groves, had been given with the intention that they would provide timber for repairs, but that Reeve had stripped the woods for his own profit.

Jackson urged Cecil to investigate the matter. Cecil did so, but the outcome could not have given either of the lessees much satisfaction. Cecil's officers found that the hospital was indeed in a sorry state of repair, with a leaking roof, a wall in danger of collapse and door-sills in need of replacement. They also found that, although there were plenty of young trees which had been left to grow on, Reeve had allowed the underwood to be badly damaged by grazing cattle, and they concluded that the lessee had no right to fell wood. Both lessees were ousted, and Thomas Thorowgood was renting the land by 1569.

Hoddesdon had been granted a charter by Elizabeth I in 1559/60 for a school to be known as the Free Grammar School of Queen Elizabeth. With the agreement of the townspeople of Hoddesdon, who had nominated the poor of the hospital, and the consent of Sir William Cecil, the hospital was closed and the buildings were used for the Grammar School by about 1570. Repairs cost the inhabitants of the parish about £46, an expense they were later to rue. The school was backed by several of the prominent local families. Thomas Thorowgood was the first bailiff and guardian; his brother, John, was one of the assistants, as were two William Sharnbrookes (Senior and Junior), Thomas Bowle who held land in Hoddesdon and Hailey, and William Garnet of Broxbourne Mill. The first schoolmaster was Philip Gerrard, but by 1574 George Birkett was in charge.

The charter granted the tolls from the market and fairs for the maintenance of the school. This gave additional validity to Hoddesdon's right to its market and fairs, and effectively brought to an end the dispute with Hertford. It should also have put the school on a sound financial footing because the

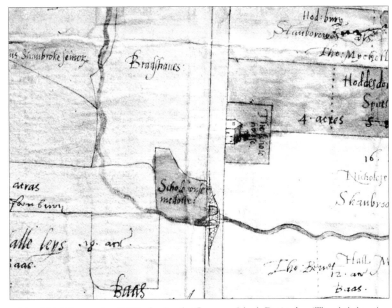

34   Detail from map c.1570, showing the Grammar School. Depicted as 'The schole house', it stood on the right of the road just north of Spital Brook © The Marquess of Salisbury

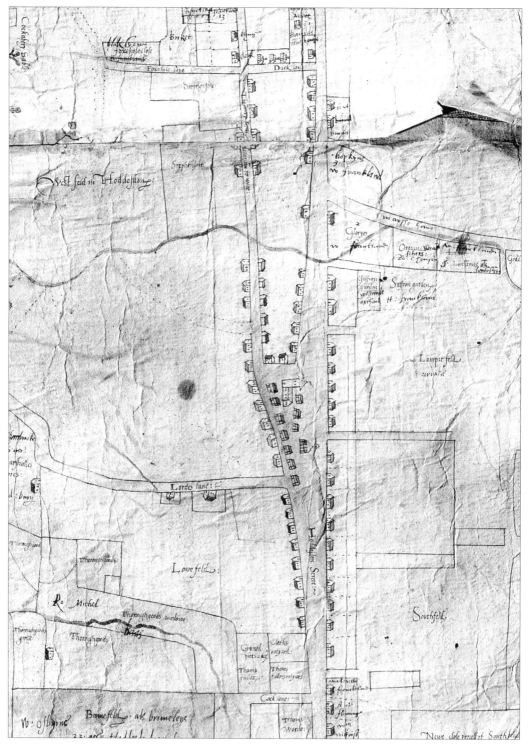

35   *Detail from map* c.1570, *showing Hoddesdon from Cock Lane in the south to Duck Lane in the north.* © *The Marquess of Salisbury*

market was flourishing in the late 16th century. There were 35 stalls and 14 'mawte shoppes' by 1585. The charter also gave the bailiff and guardians of the school considerable powers of supervision over the quality of goods sold at the market. An enquiry that Lord Burghley (Sir William Cecil) had made in 1581 seemed to indicate that the school was receiving money from the market dues, and was supported financially by most of its sponsors and others of the town. But not everything was satisfactory. A bequest to the school left by Thomas Bowle, who died in 1563, lapsed when a subsequent owner of Hailey Hall disputed the legality of it. The report concluded that Lord Burghley was bearing most of the cost of maintaining the school.

George Birkett was experiencing problems with the school and its grounds in the early 1580s. In January 1582-3 he related to Lord Burghley his dealings with the governors. He had been told by them that he had been discharged, and that the school could not continue without a new building. Birkett asked Lord Burghley for a lease of the schoolhouse and grounds. In 1586 he owned a house opposite Rawdon House, and he may have carried on the school there. In addition, problems cropped up again with the woodland, Spittle Grove. Large quantities of hazel rods were stolen in 1582, and Birkett enrolled the help of the constable. They made a search of the town and discovered caches in the loft of William Mune, the wheelwright, and in William Smyth's house. Mune denied his hazels came from Spittle Grove, but Smyth's wife 'partly' confessed, although what further action was taken is not known. Wood was an important commodity for rich and poor alike, but the comparative wealth of detail about it at this period is probably a consequence of the detailed records kept by Lord Burghley.

The school was closed by about 1585. An appeal concerning it was sent to Sir Henry Cock in 1595. This claimed the building and land were not used as either a hospital or a school and that the 'pffittes' (profits?) had gone to Lord Burghley and his farmers for the previous ten years and more. The school was not revived, and the market dues reverted to the lord of the manor (Lord Burghley). The complaint of the inhabitants was that money for repairs to make the school building viable had come from funds for church repairs, and they were left with no hospital for poor relief, no school for their children and no refund of their money either! Given the need to validate the right to hold the market, it may be that that motive was, in the school's sponsors' minds, at least as important as the establishment of a school. It seems a shame, though, that the school had such a short and undistinguished existence.

The market, which had flourished with the trade in malt, began to decline at the end of the 16th century. Most of the malt carried for the London trade went by road until this time; but when improvements in the Lea navigation began to be made, barge traffic increased. By 1588 there was a fleet of 44 barges with a total capacity of 1,100 quarters transporting wheat and malt from Ware and Hoddesdon to Queenshythe in London. The mealmen and maltmen who had controlled the road traffic resented the loss of trade and complaints were made to Lord Burghley, but he dismissed them, saying that prices would be brought down by competition between the land carriers and the water carriers. In 1594 the barge owners of Ware led by Thomas Fanshawe brought a case to the Star Chamber claiming that inhabitants of other towns along the Lea, one of whom was William Thorowgood of Hoddesdon, were trying to monopolise the carriage of malt and other grains in order to keep up prices. The judgement was that there should be free passage on the river and that both land and water transport should continue.

In 1596 Lord Burghley's Hoddesdon tenants petitioned him about access to the Lea via the Lynch Mill and the River Lynch. The mill and the river were named from the lynch (a slope ploughed to give a series of steps) between Lampit Field and the marshes. The miller at the Lynch was not prepared to agree to their scheme without Lord Burghley's agreement, which the tenants urged him to give or the market and town would be 'utterly ruined'. Lord Burghley died in 1598 and his son, Sir Robert Cecil, was his successor in national and local affairs. At one of his courts the miller at the Lynch was instructed to open the Lynch Gap for an access road (a 'drift' way) between the town and the river. Despite these measures malt continued to bypass the town and the market gradually dwindled.

In about 1560, George Ogard, the last of the Ogards to own Rye House, had sold the manors of Rye, Hailey and Thele to William Frankland. Frankland was a London clothworker who, in February 1565/6, married a widow, Joyce Saxey. William Frankland died about 1576, leaving her life interest in his manors as well as some of his property. Joyce, née Trappes, was born in 1531, the daughter of Robert Trappes, goldsmith and royal jeweller. By her first marriage to Henry Saxey she had a son, William.

William Saxey went to Cambridge and then on to Gray's Inn to read law. Sadly, though, he died when he was only 23, killed by a fall from an unbroken horse on his way from Rye House to London. His mother was distraught, but the suggestion of an acquaintance, Dean Nowell of St Paul's, that she help other young scholars, brought her some comfort. When she died in 1587 she left the bulk of her property to found scholarships and fellowships at Oxford and Cambridge colleges. She also founded Newport Grammar School, in part funded by two small tenements in Hoddesdon, one of which, opposite the end of Cock Lane, was known as Newport Cottage.

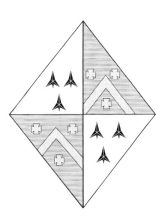

36 *Arms of Joyce Trappes. She was married first to Henry Saxey, and then to William Frankland who owned Rye House. The badge of Newport Grammar School combines the arms of Trappes and Frankland.*

Poverty and vagrancy were continuing problems. Following the dissolution of the monasteries care of the impotent poor became a parish responsibility; the able-bodied had to work and severe penalties were imposed on those who refused and on vagrants. In 1563 a Poor Law ordered the appointment of collectors to gather the charitable alms of the parish, and in 1572 the office of overseer of the poor was created. From 1597 parishes were empowered to levy a poor rate, and paupers were to be provided with work. In Hoddesdon, a poor house, or House of Correction (later called the Spinning House), was established in 1598. It stood opposite the end of Marsh Lane (now called Essex Road). It contained a block to beat hemp, one of the menial tasks often provided for the poor.

V

Early to Mid-Seventeenth Century

We have more details of life in the first half of the 17th century in Hoddesdon than for most other periods. There are thumbnail sketches about the lives of people who lived in the northern part of Hoddesdon ('Hoddesdon End' in the parish of Amwell) because the vicar of Amwell, Thomas Hassall, wrote notes about his flock in his parish register, along with details of tithes and perambulations. Two manuscripts of the Rawdon family written almost contemporaneously have also been preserved.

After the death of Elizabeth I, in March 1603, King James felt secure enough to spend nearly two months making his way from Scotland to London, being entertained and indulging his love of hunting on the way. One of his stopping places was Broxbournebury, where he was entertained by Sir Henry Cock. James was so impressed with the possibilities of the area for hunting that in 1604 he ordered bridges to be built between Hackney and Hoddesdon over the Lea so that when he was hawking in the valley he could safely and easily cross from the Hertfordshire side to the Essex side and back again. The bridge at Hoddesdon was probably at Dobbs Weir, where the river was forded. In 1618 one Laurence Biggen claimed for two years' work at £2 a year for 'having been employed to look unto his Majesty's great bridge against Hoddesdon over the river of Lea for the preventing of common passage with carts and horses made that way by rude country people, to the continual despoil of the said bridge and gates'. No doubt the 'rude country people' were pleased to take the chance of using the bridge when

they could, because crossing by ford could be hazardous when the river was running high. However, the bridge was not maintained for long. The crossing was then by ford again until the 19th century.

Apart from the excitement of the new monarchy and the pageantry of viewing the royal entourage pass nearby, 1603 was a miserable year for the town. Plague struck in the neighbourhood during the summer and lasted until the end of the year. The lack of sanitary arrangements must have helped the spread of disease; the stream was polluted and orders had to be issued for the cleaning of ditches. There was even an order in the court rolls which declared that 'no man is to cast into the street any carryon corps but shall bury the same'. There were further outbreaks of plague in 1612 and 1625.

Life for the poor was hard. The population was increasing rapidly at the beginning of the 17th century. More mouths to feed and a series of bad harvests caused large price increases in food and goods. Anyone, landowner or tradesman, who could make a surplus to sell benefited from inflation, but those on fixed incomes who had to buy at inflated prices fared badly. The weather in general was cold and stormy. England was still in the grip of the 'Little Ice Age' and the bitterly cold winters led to many crop failures.

The wealthy often left bequests in their wills for hand-outs of food and sometimes for money to be used for the poor, but the duty of provision for them fell upon the parishes. The 1601 Poor Law Act

37   The New River.

gave the job of collecting the poor rate and acting as overseers of the poor to the churchwardens of the parish and two or more substantial landowners. By this Act there were three categories of poor: able-bodied, who were to be given work; those unable to work through age or infirmity, who were to be provided for; and those unwilling to work. And parishes, having been given the task of raising a rate for the relief of their poor, felt disinclined to use this money on the poor of other parishes. The result was that vagrants were moved on with a view to chivvying them back to a place which had proper responsibility for them. The plight of Jhon (*sic*) Wallis, 'an impotent owlde man', is related in the Amwell burial register of 1603. He was ejected from Harrow-on-the-Hill and directed towards Barford in Suffolk, but died on the road at Hoddesdon.

The death rate among the young was generally high at this time, but the country areas were considered healthier than the city. So in Hoddesdon, as in many areas in the vicinity of London, there were many 'nurse children' as well as the indigenous youngsters. Poor families could make a valuable addition to their income by fostering children from the city: Christ's Hospital children, parish bastards and the children of wealthier families, who would pay to have them raised in the country.

London had traditionally relied on the Thames for its water supplies, but an increase in population had meant an increase in pollution and disease. Various schemes were proposed to bring water to the capital from outside, and in about 1600 Edmund Colthurst put forward the idea of bringing water from Chadwell and Amwell springs to London by building a channel along the 100ft. contour. Colthurst's scheme was taken over by Hugh Myddelton, whose name is now synonymous with the New River, but Colthurst continued to work on the project. Myddelton came originally from Denbigh, but had made money as a London goldsmith and cloth manufacturer. Work began in earnest early in 1609, and was completed with an opening ceremony in Islington on 29 September 1613. The first part of the work from Chadwell, through Ware, Amwell, Hoddesdon and Broxbourne, was carried out speedily, but the work stopped at Wormley for many months from January 1610 because of objections from local landowners.

The digging of the New River altered the landscape on the eastern side of Hoddesdon: Lynch Hill and Lynch Gap disappeared, and it cut through some of the property belonging to the old hospital. Details of the actual survey were lost in a fire which destroyed all the New River Company records. Labourers working on the New River were paid 10d.

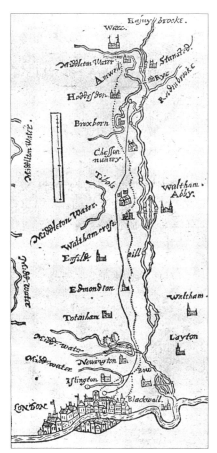

38   *Map of the New River and a rival scheme, from a woodcut of 1641 in a pamphlet supporting the scheme originally proposed ten years earlier.*

a day, with (sometimes) an extra 2d. if they were working in water. Skilled men like carpenters could earn 1s. 4d. a day and bricklayers received 1s. 6d. a day. This compared well with the agricultural labourer's average rate of 8d. a day.

Although it was many years before the New River Company made a profit, the potential of supplying water in this way was obviously seen as attractive because a rival scheme was mooted in 1631. This scheme proposed bringing water from a spring in Hoddesdon to London in a covered culvert (emphasising the cleanliness of this method as opposed to the open channel of the New River), but the plan was never carried out.

The Thorowgood Family

Continuing to prosper in the town was the Thorowgood family. William Thorowgood's family home was the Falcon on the Hoop. He had several houses in London as well as other property in Hoddesdon. He died in 1602 and his will included three charities. The first two give an indication of the provision that wealthy men were prepared to make for the poor. William's grandson, John, received three tenements (on the site where the Vicarage stands today), on condition that he gave out 26 loaves (two baker's dozens) in Broxbourne church each Sunday to 26 poor men and women of Hoddesdon and Broxbourne. To his son, John, and his heirs went property near Hertford Heath, on condition that they distributed 20 stone of steer beef and four dozen loaves to the poor of Hoddesdon on Christmas Eve each year.

The third bequest was rather different. It was to be paid by his son, Thomas, in return for property in London. Part of the money was for upkeep of Broxbourne church, part was for the preaching of six annual sermons by a 'godly' minister. Perhaps it was a sign that Thorowgood, a staunch supporter of the Reformed Church, was uneasy that Catholicism might yet have a revival that prompted him to add the proviso that the money was to be paid 'as long as the religion now established shall continue'. The will

R: White sculp

The true and lively Pourtraiture of the most virtuous Lady Elizabeth Rawdon wife to that most valliant Collonel and worthy Knight Sr Marmaduke Rawdon of Hodsden in Hartfordshire. Ætatis Suæ 76.

39 *Elizabeth Rawdon.*

specifically disbarred John Spencer, the incumbent vicar of Broxbourne. Spencer was deprived of the living of Broxbourne in 1609 for nonconformity. The executors chose Thomas Hassall, the conventionally Protestant vicar of Amwell, as a preacher to their liking. Although most of Hoddesdon lay outside his parish, Hassall was happy to oblige. These sermons led to an invitation to preach fortnightly at the chapel, which was both lucrative for him and aided his attempts to establish that the chapel lay within his parish rather than that of Broxbourne. Hassall's altercations with successive vicars of Broxbourne – to secure the patronage of wealthy parishioners and exert his rights in the matter of the chapel – continued for most of his incumbency.

William Thorowgood left his London property to Thomas and his Hoddesdon property to the family of his other son, John. Most of this also went eventually to Thomas or his heirs. Thomas Thorowgood, like William, was in the clothiery trade in London, but had a home in Hoddesdon. Where Rawdon House now stands, at the end of the 16th century there were three houses which all belonged to the Thorowgood family.

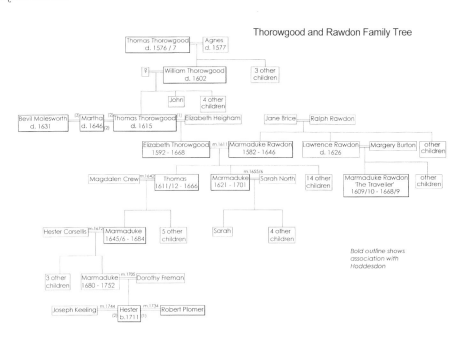

Thorowgood and Rawdon Family Tree

Bold outline shows association with Hoddesdon

In the matter of his father's bequest for the preaching of sermons, Thomas championed Thomas Hassall of Amwell, despite the fact that his dwelling lay in the Broxbourne parish part of Hoddesdon; Hassall describes Thomas as 'Mr. Thorogood, my very good friend'. As the vicar of Broxbourne, Mr Watkinson, was unwilling to let Hassall preach in Broxbourne church, the sermons took place in Hoddesdon's chapel. Although he disputed the matter, Watkinson was overruled and even advised to attend Hassall's sermons himself!

Thomas's only child was a daughter by his first wife, Elizabeth (née Heigham). Also called Elizabeth, she married Marmaduke Rawdon, a successful merchant. After the death of his first wife, Thomas married Martha (née Dorset). He died in 1615, and among his bequests was one to the poor. He left 'to the poore of the towne of Hoddesdon fower nobles a yere of currant English money to be paid for ever by meine heires and executors out of the rent of the Tenement where Gilderson now dwelleth'. The tenement was an inn, the *Cock*, owned by Thorowgood, which stood where the Grange is now situated.

The Molesworth Family

After Thomas Thorowgood's death his second wife, Martha, married Bevill Molesworth. Molesworth owned Harveys, which stood on the site now occupied by the police station (this site was previously Bradshaws, and later Woodlands). When he died in 1631, Molesworth left a bequest that the rent (50s. a year) from some of his property in Broxbourne should be used to pay 20s. to the vicars of Broxbourne to preach a yearly sermon for ever in commemoration of him and to distribute 20s. among the poor attending these sermons (thereby presumably ensuring a good attendance). The remaining 10s. was to be used to maintain the property and for 'faire and decent maintayninge of the pavements in the church about the said stone under which my body shall lye buried'. This stone was the one under which his son, also called Bevill, was buried. It bears a brass with his

coat of arms and a verse proclaiming their reunification in death.

The terms of the bequest relating to the sermon were not adhered to by his widow, Martha, who gave the commission to her favoured preacher, Thomas Hassall of Amwell. The non-payment of both this and William Thorowgood's sermon money to the vicars of Broxbourne was reported by a parliamentary commission in 1649. Martha Molesworth had died in 1646, and Elizabeth Rawdon, her stepdaughter and executor, was eventually required to make good deficiencies and arrears for both the charities despite the sequestrations and other troubles the family suffered during the Civil War.

The Rawdon Family

Born in Yorkshire in 1582, Marmaduke Rawdon went to London at the age of 17, where his older brother, Lawrence, found him a position with a merchant, Daniel Hall. He acted as a representative in Bordeaux for Hall and other merchants before returning to settle in London in 1610, where he was a member of the Clothworkers' Company. His ventures must have been highly successful for him to be in a position to pay court to an heiress like Elizabeth Thorowgood. It has been said that her dowry was £10,000, an enormous sum in those days. The couple were married in Broxbourne church in 1611.

After Thomas Thorowgood's death, Marmaduke and Elizabeth Rawdon built a new house in Hoddesdon. The house, of red brick, was known then as Hoddesdon House, and is now called Rawdon House. The date 1622 is recorded on a plaque in the brickwork of the house, but that may have been added during a later renovation. There is some evidence of a slightly later construction date. It was built with a transverse hall and a single stairway projecting from the rear (or east front). Some of its features may have been influenced by Hatfield House, which had been built a few years earlier. The Rawdons were acquainted with the 2nd Earl of Salisbury, and he and his family hunted in Hoddesdon Woods with the Earl. Rawdon House had its own water supply,

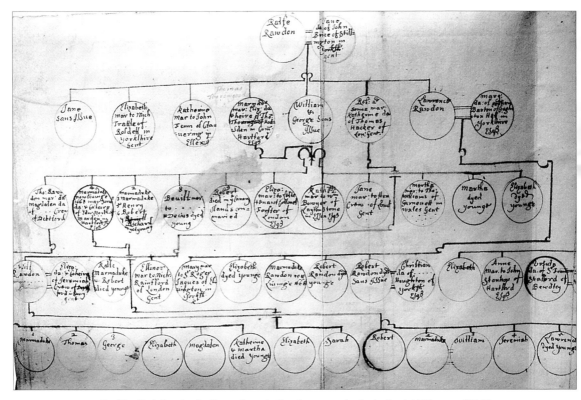

40   *Detail of Rawdon family tree from the Rawdon manuscript book, dated 1667.* HALS 79959x

piped from a spring in Godes Well Acre to the north of Lord Street over half a mile away, another indication of the wealth of the Rawdons.

Marmaduke and Elizabeth Rawdon had 16 children, eight of whom died young. The oldest son, Thomas, born in 1612, and Marmaduke, the second surviving son, born in 1621, are the only two of their children to play much part in the story of Hoddesdon. Their cousin, also called Marmaduke and born in 1610 (later known as 'the Traveller'), was adopted by the family in 1624 on the death of his father and spent some of his life in Hoddesdon.

Marmaduke (the elder) Rawdon was a man of many parts. In the City of London he became master of the Clothworkers' Company, acted as treasurer for the French merchants, and was appointed as captain of one of the City's Trained Bands (a kind of part-time home guard, paid for by a levy on those of sufficient means). He was a member of the

Common Council of the City and according to his nephew's memoirs was favoured and consulted by both James I and Charles I. He 'had often private discourse concerning several affairs of the Nation and King James wd [would] often call at his house at Hodsden coming from Royston and there had pleasant conversation together'. There is also a story that King James sometimes joined hunting parties in the Earl of Salisbury's woods when he was staying at Theobalds, and occasionally visited Rawdon House after the chase. Elizabeth Rawdon is said to have had a 'smoking room' (later called the summer house) built in the garden of Rawdon House, so that anyone wishing to smoke during the king's visits could repair to there and so not offend the king, who hated the habit.

Rawdon was a merchant adventurer: he invested in the New River; put money ($£10,000$ according to his nephew) into plantations in Barbados; sent out

The true and lively Portraiture of that most Valliant Collonel and worthy Knight Sr Marmaduke Rawdon Governour of Basing and afterwards of Faringdon for King Charles the first and died besieged in Faringdon 28th Aprill 1646.

41   Sir Marmaduke Rawdon.

42   Rawdon House.

ventures to France, Spain, the Canaries, Turkey, and the West Indies; and financed a ship to seek the North-West Passage (or find a seaway to the north of America leading to the Pacific, a popular quest at that time). He was elected as Member of Parliament for Aldborough in 1627 and was one of the Lieutenant-Colonels of the City of London in 1639. He took an interest in his home town as well, of which more later.

The growing rift between King and Parliament from the late 1630s signalled the end of a way of life for many. Marmaduke Rawdon was a staunch Royalist, but his friend the Earl of Salisbury, although initially wavering, opted finally to support Parliament. When the City of London started to side with Parliament, Rawdon, unable to sway them to his point of view and beginning to come under suspicion, relinquished his position of Lieutenant-Colonel.

He returned to Hoddesdon, put his affairs in order, and in 1643 left to join the king at Oxford. Rawdon financed the formation of an infantry regiment, and went on to command the garrison at Basing House. He withstood sieges of the house by William Waller for which he was knighted by Charles I. He returned to Basing and commanded the garrison through further sieges by Fairfax, but was later relieved of that command because of

43   Arms of Marmaduke Rawdon, from the Rawdon manuscript book, dated 1667. When Rawdon was knighted 'a rose gules in a canton or' was added to the arms. HALS 79959x

differences with the owner, the Marquis of Winchester. Basing fell soon after Rawdon's departure. He went on to defend Farringdon in Berkshire in 1645, and held it despite repeated attacks by the Parliamentary forces. It was at Farringdon that he became ill and died in April 1646. He is buried in Farringdon church.

Thomas, his eldest son, who had married in 1642 and lived at Rawdon House, had remained at home to take care of the family's affairs when Marmaduke went to Oxford. Many families took this step, essentially hedging their bets, hoping that, whatever the outcome, the family member left at home would be seen as a 'neutral', and there would be less chance of crippling penalties being imposed by the victor. Thomas, however, did not remain at home for long. In June of 1643 he too went to Oxford, where he commanded a cavalry troop.

44   Thomas Rawdon.

He does not seem to have had much luck in his subsequent affairs. He was sent as envoy to Portugal but did not secure the post of Consul which had been promised to him. Eventually, after the Commonwealth had been established, he left England in 1651, having been warned that he was in some danger. He travelled to Barbados where he found that the family property had been usurped. He was dogged by ill health and, having returned to England, was arrested in Majorca on his way back to Barbados. When he finally reached Barbados again, he learned of the Restoration and so came back to England in 1662! He attempted to get restitution from the court for losses incurred in Charles I's time, but to no avail. He returned to Hoddesdon but, after another spell in Barbados, he died of a fever in 1666 and is buried at Broxbourne.

Marmaduke (the Traveller), nephew of Sir Marmaduke, spent much of his life abroad from 1627. From 1631 he managed his uncle's estates in Tenerife in the Canary Islands, but was back in Hoddesdon in 1638. While he was there he related that his uncle 'made att his house att Hodsden a greate feaste, to which was invited Lord Salisbury and his Countess, the Lord Cranbourne his son … and several other persons of honour … and cost one hundreth and fortie pounds'. This is a staggering amount for one meal when compared with the income of a labourer earning perhaps the equivalent of 5p a day. Marmaduke also enjoyed 'buckhuntinge, sometimes in Hodsden woods' with his uncle and the Earl of Salisbury. After a year he returned to the Canaries and remained there until war with Spain enforced his departure, and he travelled back to England in 1656.

Marmaduke, second son of Sir Marmaduke, spent two spells in the Canary Islands with his cousin before the outbreak of the Civil War; the first of these trips was in 1635 when he was only fourteen. Later, when he was living in London, he contrived to send arms, powder and other supplies to his father, who was then defending Basing House. When his activities were in danger of becoming known to the

The true and lively Pourtraiture of Marmaduke Rawdon sonne of that worthy Gentleman Lawrence Rawdon late of the Cittie of Yorke Alderman he was borne in York the 17th of March Ano Dom 160⅖

45   Marmaduke Rawdon (the Traveller).

The true and lively Pourtraiture of Marmaduke Rawdon of Hodsden Esquier seacond son to that valliant Collonel and worthy Knight Sr Marmaduke Rawdon of Hodsden He was borne in London 16th August 1621.

46   Marmaduke Rawdon, son of Sir Marmaduke.

Parliamentary forces, he paid a fleeting visit to his mother in Hoddesdon and then left England to rejoin his cousin in Tenerife. He remained there until 1656, when the cousins travelled back to England together.

Back in Hoddesdon, Marmaduke set about having a house built for himself. This building, the Grange, set on the corner of Cock Lane, was completed in 1659. Whatever depredations and sequestrations the family had suffered during the Civil War, they must have retained at least some of their considerable wealth to build such a large house. In the same year Marmaduke married Sara North of Marden and brought his bride to live in the new house. The site was owned by his mother, Elizabeth, but was left to him in her will. The house received water from the Rawdon House supply. Marmaduke Rawdon lived at the Grange until his death in 1701. He gave a home to his cousin, Marmaduke the

47   Shoes, c.1660, found in the Grange.

Traveller, with whom he had sought refuge during the Civil War. This Marmaduke died in Hoddesdon in 1668 shortly after a fall from a horse.

Elizabeth Rawdon remained at Rawdon House during the Civil War. Her daughter Elizabeth and her husband, Lieutenant-Colonel Forster, were with her after Thomas left for Oxford. Thomas's son, yet another Marmaduke, was entrusted to her care soon after his birth in 1646. He was put out to nurse until he was 18 months old, but then lived with his grandmother until he went to school when he was eight. Life must have been difficult for this Royalist family living in a predominantly Parliamentarian area, and the house was plundered on at least one occasion by Parliamentary soldiers, but Elizabeth must at least have felt safe enough to remain in the area. Her son, Thomas, returned from abroad to live with her after the Restoration and her grandson, Marmaduke, also lived at Rawdon House from 1667 after his father's death, then being heir to the house. Elizabeth died in 1668, aged seventy-six.

The period up to the Civil War

The Rawdon family were not merely City gentry with a house in the country for recreation. The first Marmaduke Rawdon took a considerable interest in Hoddesdon. When he had installed the water supply for his house, it was found that there was more than sufficient and a pipe was laid from Rawdon House to the centre of the town to supply water to the townspeople. Rawdon had a statue erected, the 'Samaritan Woman' (although she has been called 'The Good Samaritan', 'Diana' and 'a nymph with an urn' by various authors). The water flowed from her urn into a pond, giving a much cleaner, more accessible supply than that which the townspeople had previously drawn from local wells, which could easily be contaminated.

Robert Cecil, 1st Earl of Salisbury and trusted Secretary of State to both Elizabeth I and James I, died in 1612. He had built a courthouse in Hoddesdon in the yard of the *Black Lion Inn* in about 1610. He was succeeded by his son, William. This 2nd

48   *The Samaritan Woman statue in the garden beside Lowewood.*

Earl of Salisbury held no major state appointments, but lived the life of a country gentleman with a passion for hunting and hawking. Part of his inheritance was land and manors in and around Hoddesdon, and he received tolls from the market and fair. With his friend and hunting companion, Marmaduke Rawdon, he was involved in the building of a Market House for the town. The Earl of Salisbury, as lord of the manors, gave his consent when petitioned by the townspeople for the building, contributed 'a great deale of tymber out of his woods neere adjoyninge' himself, and arranged for a collection to made among the inhabitants of the town and the users of the market. Rawdon gave his advice and assistance together with forty pounds towards finishing it.

Until 1616 the market had been entirely within the parish of Amwell, and the vicar of Amwell, Thomas Hassall, considered that the petition to build the new Market House (or Town House, as it was originally called, having open arcades for the market with a meeting room above) was a ploy by the people of Broxbourne to remove the trading to their own parish. He asserts that when the Earl of Salisbury's officers came to measure out the land, they did so

49   *The old court house, built c.1610 by Robert Cecil, sketched here shortly before it was demolished in 1850.*

firstly on the ancient market area, but were then influenced by the men of Broxbourne and moved the site, so that the Market House was built just south of Lord Street, on the east side of the road – in Broxbourne territory. The building was completed sometime between 1616 and 1634 when Thomas Hassall referred to it in his perambulation as 'the new Town House'.

Until Thomas Hassall became vicar of Amwell, in 1600, the chapel in Hoddesdon had been neglected for many years. It had been used as a schoolroom, storeroom, meeting room and had even been invaded by the butchers' stalls which clustered around it. Hassall took on the task of restoring it to a functional chapel, enlisting the assistance of his patron, Marmaduke Rawdon. The Rawdon family motto 'Magna est veritas et prævalet' (Truth is great and will prevail) was inscribed on the repaired chapel.

The chapel remained in use during Hassall's incumbency, al-

though it probably suffered damage from troops passing through the town. In 1649 a parliamentary commission investigated the possibility of making the chapel, which was said to lie partly in Broxbourne and partly in Amwell, into a parish church for the town of Hoddesdon. Nothing came of this at the time, probably to the great relief of both Amwell and Broxbourne parishes who derived much of their income from urban Hoddesdon.

Rawdon House was not the only large house to be built in the first half of the 17th century; Stanboroughs was erected in the centre of the town and Yew House on the southern outskirts. The Mitchells had long been the tenants of the site where Stanboroughs stands. In 1605 the tenant was Robert, grandson of the Robert Mitchell who had been involved in the court of Star Chamber case. The Mitchells had been butchers for some generations, but by 1605 Robert Mitchell was classed as 'gentleman', and was bailiff to the Earl of Salisbury; in 1645 he, or a subsequent Robert, had become 'esquire'.

Stanboroughs was probably built, of timber and plasterwork, early in the 17th century. The brick north wing was added, on the evidence of dated rainwater heads, in 1637. The house had a wall painting of a newel post and balustrade. This type of painting was popular in the 17th century. Where a staircase was placed against a wall, the painting opposite the real

50   *The* Bull Inn *(left) and the Market House, c.1826.*

51   Stanboroughs. The house was built c.1600 and re-fronted in the mid-19th century. The rainwater head on the north wing bears the date 1637 (inset).

balustrade gave the staircase a more balanced look. The Stanboroughs example was photographed in 1941, by which time it was no longer aligned with its staircase, and it disappeared in subsequent alterations.

Yew House (the name dates only from about 1800) was sited where Cedar Green is now, and its land is now covered by the Yewlands estate. There is no record of the date at which it was built, but there is evidence of 17th-century brickwork in a well and a water supply pipe from Rawdon House, so it probably dates to this time. It was built on land known originally as Sewalls and then Willifrets. In the 16th century there were three houses on the site held by John Borrell, who lived in one of them. These buildings were let by Sir Robert Cecil to John Bayley, and Yew House was probably built by him, or his son, also called John. The first John Bayley died in 1611 and the second in 1659; both are buried in Broxbourne church.

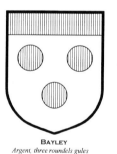

52   The arms of John Bayley.

BAYLEY
Argent, three roundels gules two and one, a chief of the last

When the Civil War broke out the majority of the local gentry supported Parliament. There was no fighting in Hoddesdon, but, as elsewhere, very heavy taxes were imposed to pay for the war. John Bayley was an active Parliamentarian who was involved in the collection of taxes in 1645. In 1649 he reported to the parliamentary commission which had been set up to enquire into church affairs and administration of charities which had fallen into disarray during the years of conflict. He reported on the state of the charitable bequests of Broxbourne parish and it was his recommendation that the old chapel could be made into a parish church for the town. Thomas Hassall, vicar of Amwell, held on to his parish during the Civil War, but Edmund Parlett of Broxbourne fell foul of the more Puritan mood and was deprived of the living in 1643.

Robert Dimsdale was another local man who worked actively for the Parliamentary cause. He was the son of a farmer, but became a barber. He seems to have had an aptitude for medicine. To become a physician required an expensive university education, but the trade of barber-surgeon required only an apprenticeship. In 1629, described as a barber of Broxbourne, he was accused of keeping an unlicensed alehouse. The following year he was indicted at the Quarter Sessions for practising the trade of grocer for which he had not served an apprenticeship, which probably means that he was selling potions and cures in addition to practising surgery. His enterprises prospered and he bought land in both Hoddesdon and Hailey. In 1631 he bought the *Dolphin* in Hoddesdon, which stood on the south corner of Lord Street. He was the tenant of a house called 'le Motes' (later the *Red Lion* inn) in Hoddesdon in 1640. Dimsdale was one of the assessors of taxes levied in Hoddesdon in 1645 for the upkeep of Fairfax's troops. Robert Dimsdale died in 1678, but several generations of Dimsdales became well known as doctors in Hertford and beyond.

VI

Mid- to Late Seventeenth Century

Thomas Hassall died in 1657, and his passing saw the end of the chapel's use as a place of worship. The next vicar of Amwell claimed that the chapel had been divested of its endowments and was not getting enough income to cover its costs. It was closed and the building left to fall into ruin.

In his book *The Compleat Angler*, published in 1653, Isaak Walton mentions the *Thatched House Inn* in Hoddesdon. The fisherman of the book meets a hunter and a falconer at Tottenham as he walks out to Ware for his fishing trip. The hunter's destination is the *Thatched House Inn* and the fisherman joins him for a rest and a drink before going on to Ware. The inn, which probably dated from about 1600, had a good reputation well before Walton's visit. In his

Tithing Book, Thomas Hassall writes of it as being 'so famous for ale and cakes'. Next to the *Thatched House* stood the *Feathers*, or *Four Feathers*. A little further south, opposite the end of Lord's Lane and standing partly in Amwell parish and partly in Broxbourne, was the *White Hart*.

The market cross was in such a bad state of repair that in 1670 a county jury considered it to be dangerous, and recommended that the inhabitants of Hoddesdon should repair it. It is not known at what date it was demolished but it may have been soon after this as the town had had the use of the market house since 1634.

Although the weather was still generally cold, warmer, drier spells during the 'Little Ice Age' were conducive to the spread of disease, and plague continued to be a problem. One such warm spell occurred in the 1660s. The plague affected London in 1665 and there were severe outbreaks in Hertfordshire in 1666, particularly affecting Hoddesdon, Cheshunt and Bishop's Stortford. A rate for the relief of the towns was levied on the county.

The Great Fire of London was said by the diarist John Evelyn to have been visible for 40 miles around, and so the glow must have been seen in Hoddesdon, an impressive if frightening sight. Christ's Hospital school in London had from

53 The Thatched House *inn.*

its earliest days sent its youngest children 'to nurse' with families living in the country close to London, mostly in Essex and Hertfordshire. After the Great Fire the movement out of London increased. There was a Christ's Hospital girls' school at Hoddesdon from 1675 to 1697. A report of 1683 stated that the mistress, Miss Harrison, had hired a house in which to teach the girls, but the location of this schoolhouse is not known. Miss Harrison was to receive 3d. a week to teach her pupils to read and sew.

The girls worshipped at St Augustine's, Broxbourne, where a gallery was erected for them in 1691. It seems that they were not boarded at the school because they had 'to goe at least a mile from Hod'sdon to Church and some of them half a mile or more to School'. This was one of the reasons cited in 1695 for a proposed move of the girls to the Christ's Hospital school at Hertford, which had spare capacity. The move was deferred when the 'Nurses' – the local people who boarded the girls – appealed at the loss of income at short notice. In 1697 the girls, 43 of them at this time, eventually left Hoddesdon for Hertford. Although they were soon moved to London, the Christ's Hospital School for Girls was permanently established at Hertford in 1778 and remained until the 1980s.

Samuel Pepys mentioned in his diary that in May 1668 he had travelled through Hoddesdon. He was going towards London 'avoiding the bad way in the forest by a privy way which brought us to Hodsden; and so to Tibald's [Theobalds]'. The privy way would have been the private toll road past Rye House.

Broxbourne and Hoddesdon were separated for rating purposes from 1666. A rate book exists from 1692, which distinguished Broxbourne proper from the hamlet of Hoddesdon; and from 1695, and possibly earlier, churchwardens for Hoddesdon were elected at separate vestries from those of Broxbourne. Vestries had, in general, taken over many of the functions of manor courts during the 16th and 17th centuries. Vestry meetings for Hoddesdon were called at Broxbourne church, but the actual meeting was often held in Hoddesdon in one of the inns of

54 Constable's staff, approximately 15cm in length.

the town. The vestry appointed the public officers of the parish such as the parish clerk, the churchwardens, the overseers of the poor and the surveyors of the highways. Constables were also usually appointed by the vestry, but it was not until 1842 that this was made a legal right, although by then the establishment of a national police force had largely superseded their functions. In Hoddesdon, the yearly appointment of a parish constable ceased in 1872. A small 'staff', the Hoddesdon constable's badge of office, with the date 1667 scratched on the ferule, is now kept at Lowewood Museum.

Care of the poor continued to be a problem for parishes. The Act of Settlement of 1662 codified a practice that had been the norm for many years: that a parish was responsible for its own poor and was not obliged to take on the burden of supporting those who came from other parishes. Persons seeking to establish residence could be challenged by the overseers of the poor within 40 days of their arrival and removed unless they could prove that they would not be a burden on the parish. In 1685 a letter from

To the Church-wardens and Overseers of the Poor of the
Parifh of *Broxborne* — — — in the County of
Hertford — and to the Church-wardens and
Overfeers of the Poor of the Parifh of *Wormley* —
in the County aforesaid or to Either of them

WHEREAS Complaint hath been made by you, the Church-
Wardens and Overfeers of the Poor of the faid Parifh
of *Broxborne* — — — unto us whofe Hands and Seals are
hereunto fet, Two of his Majefties Juftices of the Peace (*Quorum
unus*) for the County aforefaid, that *Josias Haifh and* —
Hanna his wife have — — lately intruded *themselves* — — into your faid Parifh of
Broxborne there to inhabit as Parifhioner contrary to
the laws relating to the Settlement of the Poor, and are there likely
to become Chargeable, if not timely prevented. And whereas upon due Examination and Enquiry made into the Premiffes *by the
oath of the faid Josias Haish* — — it appears
unto us, and we accordingly Adjudge, That the faid *Josias Haish
and Hanna his wife are*
likely to become chargeable unto the faid Parifh of *Broxborne*
— — and that the laft Legal Place of Settlement of the faid
Josias Haish — was in the faid Parifh of *Wormley* — —

THESE are therefore in his Majefty's Name to Order and
Require you the faid Church-wardens and Overfeers of the Poor of
the Parifh of *Broxborne* — aforefaid, That you, or fome
of you do forthwith remove and convey the faid *Josias Haish and
Hanna his wife* from your faid Parifh of *Broxborne*
to the faid Parifh of *Wormley* — — and them deliver
to the Church-wardens and Overfeers of the Poor there, or fome or
one of them, together with this our Warrant, or Order, or a true
Copy hereof, whereby they are likewife requir'd in his Majefties
Name, and by Virtue of the Statutes in fuch Cafe made, forthwith
to receive the faid *Josias Haish and Hanna his wife*
into their faid *parifh* — — and provide for *them*
as their own Parifhioner. Given under our Hands and Seals, the
7th — — Day of *Febuary* *Anno Regni*
nuni Magnæ Britanniæ, &c
Annoq; Dom. 172 8/9

*55 Document
(1728/9) empowering
the churchwardens and
overseers of the poor
of Broxbourne to
remove Josiah and
Hanna Haisham
from the parish in
accordance with the
Settlement of the Poor
regulations.*

Printed for *Henry Plowman*, at the *Plough* in *Cheapfide*, near the *Poultry*.
Where are Sold all Sorts of B L A N K S.

Sir Henry Monson to John Chauncy illustrated such a case; part of the problem was that the poor were obliged to move around in order to find work. Thomas Smyth had arrived in Broxbourne, and remained there for some time, although the parish officers ordered him to leave. He eventually moved to Hoddesdon, found work and lodging with a Robert Cooke for seven weeks and then went on to Hailey where he helped with the harvest. After another seven-week spell in Hoddesdon, he got married at Broxbourne and he and his wife moved down to Cheshunt. The Cheshunt authorities objected and sent him back to Hoddesdon, which claimed that he had actually only worked for one week there. It seems he may then have been chivvied from Hoddesdon to Broxbourne because the case was settled with an order that he was to be returned from there to Hoddesdon.

Restoration of the monarchy in 1660 must have brought relief to beleaguered Royalists, although many, like Thomas Rawdon, never recouped their losses. On the other hand, aspects of Charles II's rule caused problems for some. The Act of Uniformity of 1662 restored the Anglican faith in its entirety, and those who could not accept some of the phrases and ceremonies of the Book of Common Prayer formed various groups of nonconformists or dissenters.

The Rye House Plot

The Rye House Plot of 1683 was a plan to waylay and kill Charles II and his brother James as they returned from Newmarket, using the 'privy' way past Rye House. One of the principal characters was Richard Rumbold of Rye House. Rumbold was born about 1622. He joined the Parliamentary Army at the beginning of the Civil War and served under

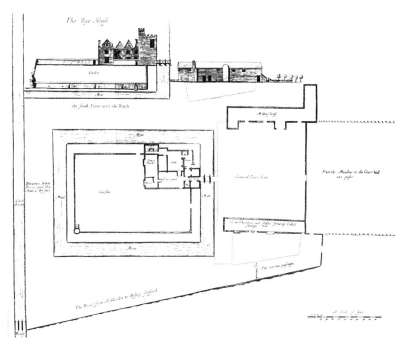

56   Plan of Rye House, 1685, from The History of Rye House Plot. *The plot was to involve the ambush of the royal coach in the narrow passage (bottom right).*

Fairfax. He was one of the guards round the scaffold at Charles I's execution, and fought at Dunbar (1650) and Worcester (1651) against Charles II. After the Restoration he married a maltster's widow, leased Rye House and took up the trade of maltster there. He was a religious dissenter, or nonconformist, who attended the Cheshunt meeting, and was named in 1682 on a list of some of the wealthiest dissenters in the parish of Cheshunt.

The Rye House Plot never materialised and was only brought to light by informants who claimed that it was not carried out because of a change in the king's plans. A fire in his Newmarket lodgings caused his party to return to London earlier than expected and the conspirators were said not to have been ready. While there may have been much talk of insurrection and methods of disposing of the king and the duke amongst discontented republicans, the evidence for the concrete action outlined came only from informants, and the 'plot' gave Charles II an excellent opportunity to rid himself of political enemies. The Earl of Essex was arrested and committed suicide,

57   The building which housed the Friends Meeting House in Marsh Lane (Essex Road) from 1679 until 1829.

or possibly was murdered, in the Tower; Lord William Russell, Algernon Sidney and many others were executed; the Duke of Monmouth went into hiding, although, because he remained a favourite of the king, little effort was made to capture him.

Of the lower ranking 'conspirators', one who was executed, Walcot, had, like Rumbold, been a guard at Charles I's execution, and had even been suspected of being the executioner. These were men who were obvious suspects either in a real or a trumped-up conspiracy. Rumbold escaped to Holland, but became involved in Monmouth's rebellion of 1685, when he joined the Earl of Argyle's invasion of Scotland. He was captured and executed in Edinburgh. Before he died he denied being involved in planning to murder the king.

Rumbold had had some sympathy among local people: an order for the arrest of a Broxbourne man, John Leonard, was issued in July 1683 because he had spoken out in vindication of Rumbold and had said he was an honest man; a list of complaints against a Cheshunt dissenter, Thomas Medlicott, in 1684 included the fact that he had been 'a great and constant companion' of Rumbold; and one of the 'teachers'

of the Cheshunt meeting, William Carstairs, was questioned on suspicion of being involved with Rumbold.

In those unsettled times all religious dissenters were viewed with much suspicion. In February 1682/3, the first known meeting of the Quakers or Society of Friends in Hoddesdon resulted in convictions for unlawful assembly for the participants with fines of 5s. imposed. Other meetings followed later that year, and in 1684 and 1685, all attracting financial penalties for those involved. John Fisher of Hoddesdon was prosecuted in 1682 for running a school without a licence from the Bishop of London. Later that year he was imprisoned in Hertford Gaol for refusing to take the oath of allegiance and was still in prison in 1686. His wife Sarah continued to attend the Hoddesdon meetings during this time. Harassment of Protestant nonconformists did not relent until 1689, when they were allowed to license their meeting houses for public worship. In 1697 John Borham, a Hoddesdon husbandman who was one of those fined in the 1680s, and Martha Pank, a widow of Broxbourne, obtained land in Marsh Lane and built a Friends Meeting House there. John Borham was appointed overseer of the poor in 1697-8.

VII

Eighteenth Century

The 18th century was a period in which national affairs played little part in the life of Hoddesdon, and the town's story is of local individuals' successes and problems, pleasures and sorrows. The difficulties of dealing with the poor continued, and the desire not to accept any more cost than necessary led to some callous decisions. In 1711 George Page was removed from Broxbourne parish to Amwell parish 'to prevent charge, in a wheelbarrow att the Point of Death for he Dyed in it'.

The poor of Hoddesdon were housed in the Spinning House or the almshouses. The very young and the old and infirm went into the almshouses. Some attempt was made to educate the young children and one of the accounts lists:

> pd for a primer for on of ye gearles 3d
> pd Mr Chery for skooling 4 children 8d

Those capable of working, including the older children, were placed in the Spinning House. There had been 14 children in 1691, and 17 in 1692. In 1700 the vestry decided that the 'parish being opprest with poor children therefor to employ the poor it is agreed to borrow twenty pounds upon the said Parish accounts. Isaac Clinton and John Coulson to manage the said work.' Coulson had also been one of those in charge in the 1690s. The managers' income was derived from the work produced by the inmates.

Vestry minutes give some indication of how the scheme worked. In 1705 two women, Susan Singlton and the Widow Walor, took on eight boys and girls for their work alone, and received 9d. a week for

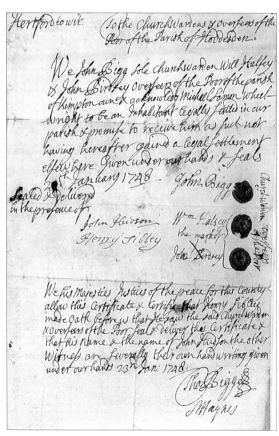

58 *Document to the churchwardens and overseers of the poor of Hoddesdon from the overseers of Kimpton acknowledging responsibility for Michael Sam if he were unable to gain legal settlement elsewhere.*

nine other children in addition to their work. These must have been younger children, presumably less skilful, and in addition having two hours a day of schooling, being taught to read. The women received 1s. 6d. a week for the youngest children (who had previously been 'at nurse'), until they could spin, with the fee dropping to 1s. after six months. In the following year the women were receiving 8d. a week and the proceeds of their work for the biggest children, but neither of these entries gives the actual ages of the children.

Under an Act of 1679, the adult poor who received outdoor relief were supposed to wear a letter P with the initial of their parish sewn to their clothing. Many parishes did not insist on this, but in 1710 the Hoddesdon vestry ordered three dozen brass badges. The poor were supposed to wear their badges at all times, with the threat of losing a week's benefit for each time a badge was not worn. More badges were bought in 1719 with the letters 'HP' on them.

From 1722, parishes were allowed to contract out care of the poor for a fixed fee. The *Dolphin Inn*

(later to be the *Five Horseshoes*) in Stanstead Valley was used as a workhouse from 1733. John Fisher and his wife were the first to run the workhouse, and received 1s. 6d. per person per week. In 1737 extra premises on the site, a house with a barn and garden, were hired from Robert Plomer in exchange for the almshouses. George Clark was the next master and the rate increased to 1s. 8d. The master was expected, as for the Spinning House, to provide materials for spinning, spinning wheels and beer. The workhouse premises were bought from Plomer's executors in 1745, and the almshouses were made into separate houses for poor families. The old Spinning House was still held as a tenancy.

George Clark remained as master until the 1750s, when Isaac Burnap took over. He received £160 per annum. His trade was flax-dressing, so presumably the inmates then worked at this rather than spinning.

In 1759 John Grapes, a silk-comber, took on the workhouse and he received £200 per annum. The inmates were not allowed out without a proper mark or ticket; the practice of badging was not abolished until 1782. Another change of trade occurred in 1769 when Thomas Attwood, a wool-comber, took over.

A Sunday Charity School was started by subscription in 1791. The children attended from 8 a.m. in summer and 9 in winter, had a break for lunch, reconvened at 2.30 and worked through till 6 o'clock. They also attended morning and afternoon services. The teachers received 1s. per 20 children and were to have an assistant 'when the number required it'.

Smallpox was a problem in Hoddesdon in 1769. In July the vestry discussed inoculation of the poor and consulted Baron Dimsdale

59 *Map of Hoddesdon in 1850 drawn by J.A. Tregelles. The almshouses were just east and north of the market cross and the workhouse was in Burford Street.*

on whether it was appropriate to inoculate in the summer months. His opinion was favourable and the vestry decided to offer inoculation to the poor, the apothecary's expenses being met by subscription. Baron Thomas Dimsdale was a great-grandson of Robert Dimsdale, the barber-surgeon of Hoddesdon, who had published several papers on inoculation against smallpox. His fame spread to the extent that in 1768 he was invited to inoculate Catherine the Great and her son, for which he was made a Baron of the Russian Empire.

One Hoddesdon boy who started life 'on the parish' prospered and did his bit to help the less fortunate in his home town. William Game was a parish apprentice in 1775. When his term of one year was over, he went to London and succeeded well enough to leave £500 to the charity school of Hoddesdon in his will of 1845.

January 25th, 1791.

WE, whofe Names are hereunto fet, Inhabitants and Land-holders in the Hamlet of HODDESDON and the Parifh of GREAT-AMWELL, in the County of HERTFORD, do hereby give Notice, that any Perfon or Perfons who fhall be apprehended and detected in breaking Hedges, lopping Trees, cutting Wood, damaging Timber, or ftealing and taking away any Perfon's Property within the faid Parifhes will be Profecuted as the Law Directs.

WILLIAM PEERE WILLIAMS, Efq;	JOHN HALE,
BENJAMIN ROOKE,	EDWARD BATTY,
WILLIAM WHITTINGSTALL,	HENRY PIGRUM,
GEORGE BORHAM,	JOHN ALLDRIDGE,
THOMAS JONES,	EDWARD PLUME,
SANS CHAPMAN,	MICHAEL SAMS,
WILLIAM MOORE,	JAMES CLARK,
JOSEPH SIMPSON,	WILLIAM CANNON,
WILLIAM TUCK,	ROBERT PERRY,
WILLIAM MANNING,	WILLIAM CROUCH.

61 Notice, 1791, warning that theft and damage to woods and hedges would be dealt with by prosecution.

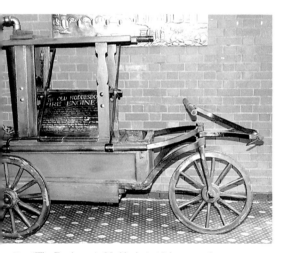

60 'The Darktown', Hoddesdon's 18th-century fire pump, now housed in the Civic Hall.

From 1710 Hoddesdon had a three-wheeled hand-drawn fire pump. The vestry was responsible for care of the fire engine and in 1738 agreed that one of the constables should be paid 10s. a year for seven years to keep it in order. In 1749 it was decided that the pump was to be tested on occasion and the men were to be allowed 2s. 6d. for beer for these practice sessions.

In 1722 the vestry ordered the construction of a cage, where petty criminals such as drunks, troublemakers and vagrants could be kept overnight and where more serious law-breakers were held until they were taken to court. Perhaps the cage mentioned in the 1534 court of Star Chamber case had fallen into disrepair. The illustration of the chapel of about 1750 (see fig.62, overleaf) seems to show a cage against the wall, and it is possible that the new cage was not built until 1761 when the vestry decided that it should be fixed to the dwelling house of John Wood or 'as neer as their Shall be no Newsence'.

By the beginning of the 18th century the chapel was falling into ruin. It had not been used for services since the late 1650s, and its last ecclesiastical use was as the venue for a vestry meeting in 1706. In 1700 one of its bells was sold to buy a clock. The verse

Parson Davis and Farmer Lock
Sold their bell to buy a clock

was related by an old inhabitant of Broxbourne to the historian Cussans, who was inclined to accept its accuracy. However, Farmer Lock remains unidentified, and the Parson Davis at that time was the Reverend Hatton Davis of Great Amwell, but the

62   The Clock House, c.1750, drawn by Charles Whitley in 1890 from an old print.

63   The Clock House, 1798, copied by Charles Whitley in 1891.

bell was still rung on Shrove Tuesdays in the 19th century. At 4 a.m. the townspeople could start to cook their pancakes and by 8 p.m. all the pancakes had to be finished, according to William Hone in his Every Day Book of 1826.

Robert Plomer was the son of William Plomer who established a brewery in the *Thatched House Inn* in Hoddesdon. The brewery, which was first mentioned in a perambulation of the parish boundaries in 1736 as 'Mr. Plomer's Brewhouse', probably dated from about 1700. William Plomer and his wife Hannah had nine children, four of whom died young. After Hannah's death, in 1715, William remarried, his second wife having the unusual Christian name of Thermuthis. William died in 1728, aged 79, and he, his first wife and several of their children are buried in the churchyard at Great Amwell. Robert took over the brewery and several inns which his father had bought. In addition, he acquired Hailey Hall and Galley Hall, as well as becoming the tenant of the Hailey Bushes estate. In 1732 he built a private chapel in Amwell Street, reputedly

vestry meeting at which the decision to replace the bell was made was held at Broxbourne church.

The chapel was altered with the building of a clock-house and a room to house a bell-ringer, and the clock was installed in 1705. Robert Plomer is said to have funded these alterations. In 1719 Jonathon Ward was employed to ring the bell at 4 a.m. and 8 p.m. – for the extinction and re-lighting of fire and candlelight. Later, the bell was also rung on special occasions such as the king's accession and the birthday of the Prince of Wales. The 'curfew'

because of a disagreement with the vicar of Broxbourne. This chapel formed the nucleus of the parish church when Hoddesdon became a separate parish in the 19th century.

In 1734 Robert Plomer married Hester Rawdon, the great-granddaughter of Thomas, eldest son of Sir Marmaduke Rawdon. She was born in 1711 and was the last of the Rawdons to be connected with Hoddesdon. The next proprietor of Rawdon House was Hannah, Robert Plomer's sister, and her husband, Thomas Smith. Robert Plomer served as High

64 *A drawing by J. Buckler, c.1830, showing the chapel built by Robert Plomer with the house of Edward Plume, saddler, on the left.*

65 *Rear of St Catherine and St Paul's church; this is the rear of the original chapel with a modern porch.*

Sheriff of Hertfordshire and died in 1740, aged fifty-two. Hester's second marriage was to Joseph Keeling in 1744. A manuscript history of the Rawdon family which came into Keeling's possession on their marriage has, strangely, had the name of Robert Plomer scratched out, although the record of his marriage to Hester and his date of death remain.

After Plomer's death, the brewery was run by René Briand, initially with a partner. Briand owned two pubs and a tap house by 1768 and acquired at least three more before his death in 1781. The business was bought by William Whittingstall, a merchant of Hitchin and also a maltster of Hoddesdon and Stanstead. In 1792 Whittingstall bought Burford House (although the house was not known by this name until the 19th century) and lived there until his death in 1803.

It was probably in this house that James Bennet, a classical scholar, ran a boarding school earlier in the 18th century. In 1761 he published an edition of the works of Roger Ascham, tutor to Queen Elizabeth I, in which he described himself as the Master of the Boarding School at Hoddesdon. A few details about the school can be gleaned from the accounts of Thomas Green. Green (1719-91), organist at All Saints, Hertford, was also a tuner of musical instruments and taught drawing and music, both privately and in schools. He kept detailed accounts from 1742 to 1790. Green taught 11 pupils at Mr Bennet's school between 1751 and 1767, and also tuned a harpsichord and a spinet there. Green's pupils at this school rarely kept up their musical studies for more than 12 months.

One of James Bennet's pupils was John Hoole (1727-1803). Bennet introduced Hoole to John Scott of Amwell when Scott's family had moved temporarily to St Margarets to avoid an outbreak of smallpox in Ware in 1761. John Hoole published a biography of John Scott in 1785. He was also a successful playwright and translator, and was acquainted with Samuel Johnson. James Bennet's son, John, was a friend of both Hoole and Scott, and it was Scott who confirmed news of John's death to another friend in a letter of 1762. There was severe flooding in the Lea valley in November of that year – Scott estimated that the river had risen nearly six feet – and John Bennet drowned in the floods. James Bennet himself died in 1777.

Yew House was another of Hoddesdon's houses to be used as a school in the 18th century. Mrs Tutty ran 'The Ladies Boarding School' there from 1755 until 1782. As Miss Hallow, she had started her school in Hertford in 1748. She married the Reverend William Tutty in 1753, and the school moved to Hoddesdon two years later. At Mrs Tutty's, Thomas Green taught seven pupils each year on average. In general, the girls persevered with their studies for much longer than Mr Bennet's boys. At least one of Mrs Tutty's pupils was from Hoddesdon itself. Miss Briand, daughter of the brewery owner, left the school

at Christmas 1764, but continued her music studies privately with Thomas Green until 1768. Then, for a few months in 1770, she was taught drawing by him. Another local pupil was Mary Prescott, daughter of George Prescott of Theobalds, who left the school in 1769, aged fourteen. The outbreak of smallpox which caused John Scott's family to leave Ware in 1761 also affected one of Mrs Tutty's girls. Thomas Green noted that Miss Neale stopped having her harpsichord lessons in that year 'being gone home to be inoculated for the Small Pox'.

Mrs Tutty's school prospered but Thomas Green seems to have had a certain amount of trouble in getting paid for his work. By 1776 the account was four years in arrears, and was not finally cleared until two years after the school closed in 1782. Several Hoddesdon families employed Thomas Green to tune instruments. Harpsichords and spinets were the most popular instruments of the time, but pianos were beginning to be available from the mid-18th century. In Hoddesdon, a Mrs Farrendon of Lords Lane and a Miss Turvin had pianos by 1781 (Lady Monson of Broxbournebury had one by 1770).

Thomas Green was also a prolific writer of verse and letters in verse. One set of 30 verses attributed to him was entitled 'The Cruel Parting or Lamentation of the Ladies of Hoddesdon upon the departure of the Worcester Militia'. The American War of Independence was being fought and the alliance of France with America prompted the calling up of the militias. The Worcester Militia was called to arms in March 1778. After a spell at Warley Common, Essex, the Worcesters moved to their winter quarters around Hertford in November 1778. Headquarters and four companies were at Hertford itself, with three companies at Ware and Wadesmill and two at Hoddesdon. Thomas Green's verses relate how the young ladies of Hoddesdon (Kitty Briand is one of those mentioned) enjoyed the months of the militia's stay

> With them to walk, with them to chat
> The time stole blythe away
> And gay Assemblies, Dances, Balls
> Clos'd evr'y joyous day.

In June 1789 the Worcester Militia left to join other units at Coxheath in Kent where they trained in readiness for a possible invasion. According to Green, the ladies of Hoddesdon were inconsolable at their departure!

Rawdon House, which had come into the possession of Hannah Smith (née Plomer), descended to her daughter, Thermuthis, in 1751. She married Richard Chamberleyne, and the house went to their son, Stanes Chamberleyne. In about 1770, when Rawdon House was unoccupied, the seats on the north side of the chancel of Broxbourne church, which seem to have belonged to the Rawdons, were

transferred to the owners of Yew House. Stanes Chamberleyne married Mary Brockett, and their son inherited Rawdon House in 1834. From 1740 the house was let to tenants, one of whom was John Dymoke, hereditary Champion of England, who was in possession from 1778-9. In the period 1771-9 there are several mentions in Thomas Green's accounts of tuning for the 'Hon'ble Champion' Dymoke and of teaching the Misses Dymoke, so it is likely either that his tenancy of Rawdon House was for a longer period than a year or that he was resident elsewhere in Hoddesdon.

John Dymoke held the appointment of overseer for the parish in 1778, and the vestry appointed George Cheffins to be his deputy. George Cheffins was a joiner by trade who was employed on the building of Sherborne House in 1760. He married and settled in the town, and his grandson was bailiff to the Marquess of Salisbury. The gate piers at the western end of the Grange property are made of soft red brick and have many names inscribed on them. On the side of one of the outer piers is a J Cheffins, and beneath it, in a different hand, is one

66 *(left)   The Grange, c.1960.*

67 *(below)   The gates of the Grange, with the Arabella Oxendon monogram over the gates and detail of Grange gate pier.*

68   Detail from 'A Topographical Map of Hartfordshire from an Actual Survey', Dury and Andrews, 1766.

69   Lowewood: front and rear views.

of the earliest inscriptions on the piers – the date 1726.

The Grange changed hands in the 18th century. Marmaduke Rawdon, second son of Sir Marmaduke, died in 1701, leaving the house to his daughter, Sarah. By 1725 the Grange was owned by Lady Arabella Oxendon. She had many alterations made and probably built the south wing. The wrought-iron gates and brick piers at the west end of the grounds were also added by her. Her monogram can still be seen over the gates, but the crest of the Rockingham family, of which she was a member, was stolen during development of the site in the late 20th century. Lady Arabella died in 1735, leaving the Grange to her sister, Eleanor, who was married to Lord Leigh. Thomas Green tuned a spinet for Lady Charlotte Montague at the 'Hon Mr Leighs' in 1745 and the following year got a commission from Mr Lee (Leigh) to paint his crest. The Grange remained in the Leigh family until 1764.

From 1764 until 1854 the house belonged to the Hughes family. The owner from 1777 until his death in 1785 was Hugh Hughes, who was a druggist by profession. The Grange was one of two houses (the other was at Waltham Abbey) to suffer from what the *Gentleman's Magazine* described as 'a new mode of burglary' in January 1781. The house was broken into and robbed by two persons in a 'one-horse chair', which was presumably the 18th-century version of the getaway car. Another house owned by Hugh Hughes was Lowewood. The name seems to have been given to this building at some time early in the 20th century. Prior to that the house does not seem to have had a specific name. The land was known as Harveys in 1570 and belonged to Jasper Garnett a century later. The present house was built in about 1760. It is possible that part of Garnett's house was incorporated into the new house, because the rear of Lowewood is different in style, the height of the ceilings being much lower. Hugh Hughes was in possession in 1780. Ownership passed to the Whitelock family in 1795. Captain Hugh Hughes and others purchased the house in 1830 and sold it to John Warner and his son in 1835.

70   *Rathmore House, with detail of the entablature below the pediment (inset).*

Rathmore House was built in 1746 by John Borham. The previous building on this site, which fell down in 1739, had been bequeathed to the guardians of St Katherine's chapel. In 1743 the ground was let by the parish to John Borham. His initials and the date in Roman numerals can be seen on the entablature below the pediment of the door of Rathmore House. This John, born in 1684, was probably the son of the John Borham who, with Martha Pank, had built the Friends Meeting House in Marsh Lane. He ran various businesses in Hoddesdon; he was a farmer, a mealman, a maltster, and held the Lynch Mill in 1740. From the mill he had access to London markets, by way of the River Lynch which joined the Lea at Hoddesdon Lock.

VIII

Nineteenth Century – Hamlet to Urban District

✧

The population of Hoddesdon increased dramatically in the 19th century, and many traditional institutions and ways of life changed. The brewery grew to become a major employer in the town by the middle of the century. In 1803 the brewery owner, William Whittingstall, died suddenly and the business was bought in 1805 by William Christie and George Cathrow for £59,401. Brewers adopting the tied house system – buying inns and alehouses to be supplied exclusively with their own products – needed large amounts of capital, and some companies, Christie and Cathrow included, acted as bankers to other breweries. They founded the Hertford Bank in Fore Street in 1807. The Hertford Bank

71   *William Christie, 1744-1811.*

suffered a substantial loss (over £3,000) in 1814 when a coach transferring notes to London was robbed and, perhaps because of this, the bank was taken over by Samuel Adams' Ware Bank later that year.

Mr and Mrs Christie were tenants of the Grange, and Mrs Christie continued to live there after William's death in 1811. Their son, John, took over the brewery with George Cathrow, and their nephew, Peter Christie, was apprenticed to the firm. George Cathrow died in 1842 and was buried at St John's, Great Amwell. His wife and two sons, one of whom had been curate of St John's, had pre-deceased him. The brewery and its inns were put up for auction but eventually were bought privately by John Back and Robert Hunt, with Peter Christie. Initially known as Hunt & Co., the firm's name changed to Christie and Hunt in 1843. They substantially increased their number of inns by taking over and closing Carter's brewery in Hertford but retaining the inns. They also rebuilt the Hoddesdon brewery.

In about 1816 Peter Christie married Ellen Louisa, the daughter of the Reverend William Jones of St Augustine's, Broxbourne. The brewery business was in the hands of their son, Charles Peter Christie, from at least 1862, taking the name C.P. Christie and Co. Robert Hunt had retired in 1860, and, soon after Peter Christie's death in 1865, John Back also retired. Charles Peter Christie enlarged the brewery and made it the biggest in the county. Within the brewery complex was a heated swimming pool. Dating from about 1890, it made use of water warmed during the process of cooling the brewing vessels. During the winter months the pool was boarded over and used for events such as concerts and plays.

C.P. Christie's home for some years was the building on the south side of Brewery Road (previously the *Thatched House Inn*), but in 1878 he built himself a house on the site of a property which had belonged to James Esdaile early in the century. Esdaile had been a tenant of Rawdon House in 1807, moving to the house which took his name some time before 1813. Christie's house kept the name, but with the spelling Esdale, possibly due to a transcription by a clerk. C.P. Christie was married to Isabel Perkins of Norris Lodge, which stood in Lord Street. He gave the recreation ground in Whitley

72 (far right)   C.P. Christie, c.1890.

73 (right)   Christie & Co. stone beer bottle.

74 (below)   Christie & Co. stone jar.

75 (below right)   Bird's-eye view of the brewery, 1897.

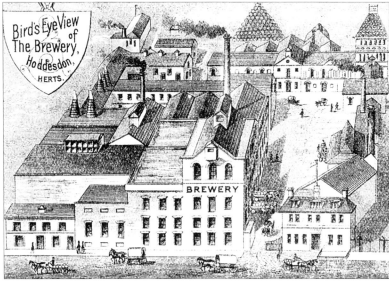

76   Esdaile House (centre), 1873. Rathmore House, which is now the end house, is the third building to the left of Esdaile House.

77   Esdale House, rear, 1906.

78   Monument to Isabel Christie in the recreation area, Whitley Road.

Road to the town in 1897 in memory of her. C.P. Christie died in 1898, aged 65, and the brewery was then run as a partnership by his four sons.

The problems of the poor were still acute in the 19th century. The Reverend Jones of Broxbourne wrote in his *Parish Register* about a serious outbreak of illness which affected Hoddesdon and other local towns early in 1802. The outbreak, in which many people died, lasted for some months in Hoddesdon. Jones noted that it was confined almost entirely to the poor, which he attributed to filthy living conditions and the fact that the poor were 'so reduced by the severe pressure of the times that they have not any thing like strength remaining which might resist or throw off distemper in any form'. He had attributed the start of the outbreak in Hoddesdon

to unwashed infected garments being brought to the town by a woman who had nursed her dying mother in Ware. The woman herself subsequently died. Jones thought that isolation of the sick, combined with the burning of clothing and fumigation of homes, would have resulted in the saving of many lives. He regretted that, although Hoddesdon had a pest-house for housing the contagious, it had not been kept for that purpose but had been let out to a family for many years. The old manor house of Geddings seems to have been the site of this pest-house.

In 1805 Dr James of High Grounds (later High Leigh) was called upon by the vestry to inoculate the poor of the town against smallpox. Dr James bought the lease of Rathmore House in 1812; it was used thereafter by many different doctors up until 1969, and was known locally as 'The Doctor's House'.

The Reverend Jones's assessment of the town's provision for the poor was not very favourable. He wrote in his diary in 1802 that the almshouses, built by Richard Rich in 1440, were in 'a most miserable confined alley'; and he thought that whilst the workhouse was not badly situated, it was much in need of repair. Neither was to be used for much longer because a Poor Law of 1834 introduced a different way of dealing with the poor. Parishes were grouped

79   Rye House, 1784. In the 18th and early 19th centuries the gatehouse was used as the parish workhouse of Stanstead Abbotts.

in unions which provided workhouses for the destitute. The poor of Hoddesdon were transferred to the Ware Union. The poor of Stanstead Abbotts, who had been housed in Rye House, were also removed to Ware.

The Hoddesdon workhouse became an inn again, taking the name of the *Five Horseshoes*. The building was pulled down in 1866 and a new inn, which lasted until 1968/9, was built keeping the same name. The almshouses were sold in 1841 to Cathrow and Christie and were subsequently demolished. The money raised was used to pay debts owed by the town and towards the cost of a lock-up and an engine house. The hand-drawn fire pump was replaced in 1853 by a larger horse-drawn vehicle. In 1897 it was decided to erect new almshouses, or

80 *The* Five Horseshoes *inn, Burford Street, c.1866.*

'Cottages for the Aged Poor', to celebrate the Diamond Jubilee of Queen Victoria. The money was raised by public subscription and donations, and three cottages were built on a site at the bottom of Rosehill given by Robert Barclay.

81 *Bust of Queen Victoria on the wall of the Queen Victoria Cottage Homes, Beech Walk. The brass gate plate is pictured below.*

Lawlessness had increased nationally in the early decades of the 19th century, perhaps because of the high level of unemployment exacerbated by the large number of men discharged at the end of the Napoleonic Wars. Highway robbery was particularly feared in the 1820s by traders who had come to Hoddesdon's market from Hertford and had to make their way home at night across Hertford Heath. Their solution was to gather in the *Black Lion*, waiting (and presumably drinking) until their number (and their courage) was sufficient for them to ride home *en masse*.

The formation of the London Police in 1829 may have solved some of the capital's crime problems, but had led to more vagrants on the roads away from the city. A spate of seven house burglaries or attempted burglaries in 1834 prompted Hoddesdon to appeal to the justices at Hertford Sessions for a county rate to be levied for the building of cells.

Many changes took place in the first half of the 19th century which altered the look of the town centre. The maypole, which stood near the chapel and had been mentioned nearly 200 years previously

82 *Illustrations from a pamphlet, 1894, for the re-erection of the Samaritan Woman at the north end of the market place.*

83 *The High Street, looking north, c.1860, showing the pump which replaced the Samaritan Woman.*

by Thomas Hassall in his Tithing Book, blew down about 1820 and was not replaced.

In 1826 the Samaritan Woman statue and the open pond into which her water poured were replaced with a pump and an underground tank. The flow of water had lessened and the enclosed tank prevented wastage of water and was also more hygienic. The statue was in a poor condition; dripping water and holes made for pipes had, according to one newspaper correspondent of the time, made it look indelicate and suggestive. It was placed in a yard on the other side of the street, and there it suffered even more damage as a target for stone-throwing boys. A pamphlet was published in 1894 proposing the re-erection of the statue near the Clock House. The plan was abandoned because of advice that the statue was too badly damaged to be renovated. The statue was at least taken into the care of the council; it was removed from the yard and stored in a building at Rye Farm, where it remained for many years.

The slope of Amwell Street was altered in 1826, making the familiar high pavement of today. During the work, the hexagonal brick foundation of the market cross was found opposite the end of Lord Street. The market house built in 1634 was demolished in 1834. Its upper room, which had been used for public meetings, entertainments and theatrical performances, was used as a public venue for the last time in December 1832. The first county election following the Reform Bill of 1832 was held there. By the 1830s the Thursday market had dwindled to nothing and so the market house had lost its primary function. In 1833 the people of Hoddesdon applied to the Marquess of Salisbury for its removal, claiming that the road between it and the *Bull* was narrow and dangerous. Their request was granted and the market house was pulled down. Six pieces of ornamental oak carving from it were given into the care of the bailiff, Caius Cheffins, and in 1846 were taken to Hatfield House to be used in the chapel there. In March 1886 a new market was started in Hoddesdon

84   *The High Street, 1811, with the* Bull *inn (left) and the market house (right). The old chapel/clock-house is visible to the right behind Middle Row. There are several versions of this print, with the dates between 1780 and 1818. Despite the impression given on this illustration the roof of the market house was intact.*

85   *The* Bull *inn and the market house, c.1830. The* Maidenhead *inn, the old chapel/clock-house and Middle Row are in the background.*

86   *The cattle market,* c.*1900.*

by Ernest Bridgeman. This was held on Wednesdays and was initially primarily a cattle market.

The fair's trading aspect had also diminished and by 1826 was described as being for toys and pleasure. It was held in the High Street until the 1890s, when it was moved, first to Amwell Street and then to Pound Close.

The old chapel/clock-house was demolished in 1835. A new building was erected, funded by public subscription and donations by the brewery owners, Cathrow and Christie, who gave 50,000 bricks, and G.J. Bosanquet of Broxbournebury, who gave 60,000. The new Clock House soon became known as the

Town Hall. It was used for vestry meetings and for those of several local societies. Two cells were built for the temporary imprisonment of vagrants and suspected criminals, and from 1842 until 1883 rent was paid by the Chief Constable of Hertfordshire for use of part of the building. In 1883 a police station was built in Lord Street. Despite the formation of the County Police, the appointment of parish constable was not discontinued until 1872. Provision was also made in the Clock House for the fire engine and its equipment. In 1853 a new fire engine was bought by public subscription.

A new clock for the Clock House was bought in

87 *The old clock-house, a drawing by J. Buckler c.1830 (left). The* Maidenhead *is to the left and the* Bell *to the right. The new Clock House, 1853 (below) shows Middle Row in the foreground.*

1870. Although the old one was said to be worn out, it was bought by C.P. Christie and stood in the brewery yard for several years. The Clock House did not find favour with all commentators. It was described in about 1905 by C.G. Harper, who wrote a series of books, *Roads*, as 'the ugly modern building that Hoddesdon folk call the Clock House; really a fire-engine house with a clock tower'. He was even less impressed by the mermaid weathervane chosen by members of the vestry, saying that it 'oddly conjoined the characteristics of a fiddler, a sagittarius and a dolphin'.

Middle Row, a block of dwellings which had evolved from market stalls and which sprawled in front of the brewery buildings, was demolished at the instigation of Peter Christie in 1857. It was not only the look of the town centre that was changing. The coming of the railway made a big impact on the life of Hoddesdon. The town's position on one of the major routes out of London meant that the livelihood of many of the inhabitants was directed towards catering for travellers. The many inns provided accommodation and stabling. By 1835 there

88 *Lord Street, c.1910; the police station is on the left.*

89 *A replacement of the original weather vane, which is in Lowewood Museum.*

90   *Lampits, c.1910.*

91   *The watercress beds and the Lynch Mill, c.1890.*

for a third-class single ticket. Passenger traffic and freight transferred to the railway, and the roads became quieter for a period. The Eastern Counties Railway took over the running of the Northern and Eastern in 1844, and this became part of the Great Eastern Railway in 1862.

The railway was built across the meads, otherwise called Lammas land. The company paid £470 in compensation for the loss of grazing rights when the main line was constructed, with a further £85 on construction of the Ware and Hertford branch. The original intention was to use the money for town lighting but it was eventually shared out amongst the 244 holders of Lammas rights.

Enclosure was late in coming to Hoddesdon. The first of the common fields to be enclosed was Lampit Field in 1841. The principal owner was James Poulter Manser, of the Lynch mill. He was allotted 14 acres, which became the Lampits property. It was the home of his son, Alfred Manser, and then of Captain Christie of the brewing family. The Lynch mill had been bought in 1803 by J.P. Manser and his brother Edward. It ceased working in 1873 and was demolished in 1892. From 1885 until 1961 the water supply was used to grow watercress. J.P. Manser built a mill at Dobbs Weir in 1830: called Charlton Mill, it was water-powered until 1856, when steam was added; it was destroyed by fire in 1868.

Manser built himself a house, the Lynch, soon after acquiring that property, and lived there until his death in 1856. His son, Henry Manser of the Lynch, was one of the victims of a train crash on the local line in 1860. The engine of the London

were four mail-coaches and 27 other stage-coaches a day. Some were for local destinations, such as Ware, Hertford and Hoddesdon itself, but many travelled further afield: to Cambridge, Peterborough, Wisbech and Lynn; to Lincoln, Hull and York.

The Northern and Eastern Railway Company received Royal Assent for their railway bill in 1836. The railway reached Broxbourne in 1840, and Bishop's Stortford in 1842; the branch line from Broxbourne to Hertford opened in 1843. The journey time from the London terminus, Shoreditch, to Broxbourne was 45 minutes and the cost was 1s. 6d.

express was derailed at Tottenham station. It partially mounted the platform and fell back on the first carriage. Several people, including the driver, were killed and Henry Manser had to have a leg amputated. He sued the railway and received £2,000 compensation. The Lynch remained in the Manser family until 1948, when it was sold following the death of Harold Manser.

After the enclosure of Lampit Field a few years elapsed before an Enclosure Act of 1855 finally ended the open field system. Arable fields, meads and marshes were all subject to the Act. The main landowners were the Marquess of Salisbury, E.W. Whittingstall, James Cathrow, G.J. Bosanquet, Charles Webb, J.P. Manser, Charles Whitley and Caius Cheffins; there were also 245 claimants of grazing rights on the meads and marshes.

Charles Whitley was a rate collector who became involved in advising on entitlement to rights during enclosure in the 1850s. His son, also called Charles, was instrumental in buying and selling land for building in the 1870s in the area later to be Rye Park (then known as Rye Common), the population of which was one thousand within 20 years. Charles Whitley, junior, was a local historian: he left many notes on the town's history and made a collection of artefacts which formed the basis of Lowewood Museum; he was also an artist who drew sketches and painted watercolours of many local scenes. He died in 1893, aged seventy.

The provision of public utilities took place from the middle of the 19th century. Oil lamps were used for street lighting in 1842. The Gas Company was formed in 1847, with gas works near Spitalfields. The first gas lamps were lit in 1848, and there were 40 public lights by 1850. In 1886 a new gas works was built close to the railway. The Sanitary District was formed in 1874 and a system of drainage was laid out in the main streets of the town. The New River Company was unwilling to provide drinking water and so the Hoddesdon Waterworks Company was formed in 1876.

The institutions of local government were undergoing change. The manor court was held for the last time at the *Black Lion* (soon to become the *Salisbury Arms*) in 1826, its function superseded by the county sessions. In 1894 the Local Government Act was passed, which divided counties into urban and rural districts. The population of the town had increased sharply in the 19th century and Hoddesdon opted to become an urban district, Hoddesdon Urban District Council taking over the duties of the

92 *The Coffin Houses. The building was demolished in 1959. Priory Close now stands on the site.*

vestry. The first clerk of the council was Alexander McKenzie, a contemporary of Charles Whitley and, like him, a local historian. He held office until 1901. McKenzie lived in the building known by its shape as the 'Coffin Houses'. It had been divided to make two houses and Yew Arbour, the southern one, was Alexander McKenzie's home. His offices abutted the house on the south, and were the council offices until 1926.

In ecclesiastical matters as well as secular, the 19th century was a time of change. In 1822 the chapel built by Plomer was bought by the people of

93   *Hoddesdon Chapel, soon to become the parish church, with the National School buildings on the left, c.1850.*

Hoddesdon. The money was raised by public subscription and a grant from the Incorporated Church Building Society. When the scheme was first mooted, in 1820, it was discovered that the chapel lay partly in Broxbourne and partly in Great Amwell. Both vicars claimed the right of presentation, and the problem was finally solved with an agreement that the chapel would be served alternately by the incumbents of the two parishes. In 1823 the building was consecrated as a chapel of ease for the parishes of Broxbourne and Great Amwell. The arrangement of dual right of presentation ended in 1843, when the decision was made to form a new district of Hoddesdon from the parishes of Broxbourne and Great Amwell. The Consolidated Chapelry District of Hoddesdon, which was assigned about 1,700 people from Broxbourne and 500 from Great Amwell, came into being in 1844. This ecclesiastical district became the parish of Hoddesdon in 1856.

By 1860 the chapel, now the parish church, was too small for the congregation. It was decided that a new church should be built, but that was found to be too expensive. The idea of extending the existing building was not popular, and was also considered too expensive, but this was the course which was finally adopted in 1864. A chancel, aisles, and south and west porches were added, as was the base of the tower. The builder was a local man, John Hunt, who was also a churchwarden. The extended building was dedicated in 1865. The records have been lost, but the Ordnance Survey map of 1880 and local directories of the time name it as the Church of St Catherine. The tower was completed in 1887. A bequest of William East given to build the tower and hang a peal of bells was not sufficient for both purposes, and the bells were added in 1901.

The Friends Meeting House in Marsh Lane was used from 1679 until 1829, when the present Meeting House in Lords Lane was built. The Independent or Congregational Church was built in the High Street in 1847.

There was a growing feeling nationally at the beginning of the 19th century that a Christian education should be provided for the children of the poor. Two societies formed which were at the forefront of this movement. In 1808 a nonconformist initiative

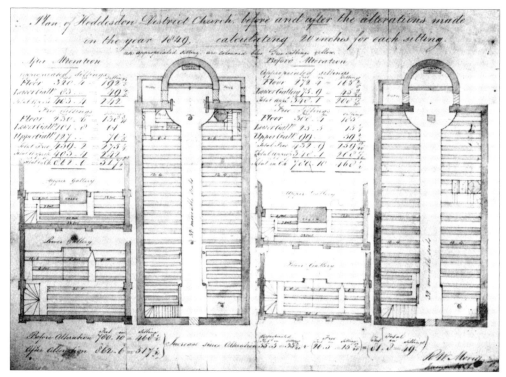

94 *A plan drawn by the Reverend William Morice, first vicar of Hoddesdon, for alterations to the chapel, 1849; the pulpit was moved from the south side to the east end and the seating was increased to 517½ places.*

95 *Hoddesdon parish church, 1880.*

led to the British and Foreign Schools Society. The
Anglican Church responded in 1811 by forming the
National Society for the Education of the Poor in
the Established Church. There were both British and
National schools in Hoddesdon.

The first charity school on record in Hoddesdon
was built in 1818 by Mrs Easter Jones, who endowed
it with £1,000. The school was situated on the eastern
side of Amwell Street, with Woollens Brook to the
north and an orchard to the south. The pupils were
poor girls of the hamlet of Hoddesdon who were to
be taught to spell, read, knit and work at the needle.
This emphasis on domestic skills was a feature of
girls' education until well into the 20th century. A
house was built for the mistress, who was paid £20
per annum. Mrs Jones may have been unsure whether

96   *Friends Meeting House, Lord Street.*

97   *Amwell Street, 1900, just north of Woollens Brook, looking north.*

the school would succeed, because she made the
proviso that, if it were discontinued, the buildings
were to be converted to houses for two women,
either spinsters or widows.

National Schools for boys and for girls (the
endowed school) are entered in a trade directory for

1832, with places for 100 boys and 50 girls
respectively. The address of the Boys' National
School was given as Stanstead Valley (now Burford
Street) in the 1839 edition. A school house and
master's house for the school were built at the west
end of Paul's Lane in 1844, through the efforts of

the Reverend Morice, first vicar of the parish of Hoddesdon. An Infants' National School was also established in Paul's Lane in 1844, and was extended in 1875. In 1846 Robert Hunt, one of the brewery owners, gave the site of a house and a malting in Pauls Lane to the vicar of Hoddesdon. The buildings were demolished and a Girls' National School and mistress's house were built in 1858. Mrs Easter Jones's school transferred to the new site and the endowment fund and proceeds from the sale of the old buildings passed to the managers of the National School.

The first British School in Hoddesdon was the boys' school, built in 1841 by John Warner, a leading Quaker in the town. The school was situated in a field adjacent to Rawdon House, which was then owned by Warner. It seems that this school only had a short life – the school's Minute Book was kept only until 1849 – and it closed once the Boys' National School was established.

The Girls' British School opened in 1844. John Warner was again closely involved, as were William Ellis, the Independent pastor, and his wife, Sarah. John Warner offered the use of a small house until a suitable place for the school could be found. In 1846 a piece of land on the site bought for the Independent Church was offered for £93 by William Ellis for the building of the Girls' and Infants' School. The offer was accepted and it was agreed that half the school's trustees would be Quakers and half Independents.

The Minute Books of the British Schools give an indication of the education received. The scholars at the boys' school were to be between five and 13 years old. School hours were from 9 a.m. until 12 noon and from 2 p.m. until 5 p.m. Holidays were one week at Christmas, with a longer break at harvest time, three weeks for the boys and a month for the girls. The timing of the summer break to coincide

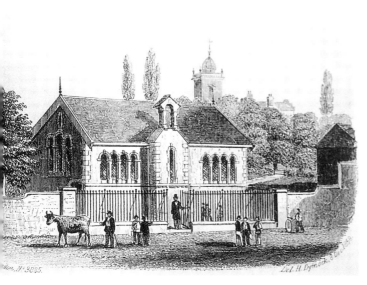
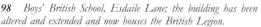

98 Boys' British School, Esdaile Lane; the building has been altered and extended and now houses the British Legion.

99 Stone over the entrance of the Boys' National School, Pauls Lane, recording the date of building.

100 Girls' National School foundation stone, now situated in the grass on the site where the building stood.

101 Foundation stone of the Boys' British School on the wall of the British Legion headquarters.

102   The Girls' British School and the Congregational Church which stood in the High Street where Fawkon Walk is now situated.

with harvest was a practical decision. Agriculture was a major employer and absenteeism would have been high if the schools had been in session. A charge of 2d. a week was made for the first child in a family, 1½d. for siblings, and 1d. for fatherless children. However, this did not represent the true cost of education. While a child was at school he or she was not earning a wage to contribute to the family's income. The level of poverty is indicated by a decision at one of the committee meetings of the girls' school to provide the pupils with capes and shawls as their school treat instead of putting on a tea with buns.

The original rules of the infants' department had included the decision to have a minimum age of two, but this seems to have been relaxed over the years. It seems that it was not uncommon for schools to take very young children, so that in effect they were crèches rather than schools. However, after a visit from school inspectors in 1858 it was decided that no new child under two was to be admitted.

Legislation in 1876 stated that all children should have elementary education and the 1880 Education Act made schooling compulsory for five- to ten-year-olds. Elementary education became free in 1891 and the leaving age was raised to 12 in 1899. The

Girls' and Infants' British Schools and the National Schools continued to provide education into the 20th century.

The Rye Common area grew rapidly towards the end of the 19th century. The name Rye Park, which was on the Ordnance Survey map of 1898, was gaining in usage. In 1880 a 'mission' church, a small corrugated iron church, was built in the Old Highway under the auspices of John Alfred Hunt of Hoddesdon and Robert Barclay of High Leigh. It was over twenty years before the church had its own curate. Before that the vicar of Hoddesdon celebrated Holy Communion on occasion and other services were taken by Robert Barclay and John Hunt. St Cuthbert's church was built in Whitley Road in 1908. A National Infants' School was established in Rumbold Road in 1892.

The railway line to Hertford opened in 1843, but no station was built at Rye House because there was no community to serve at that time. In 1845 the proprietor of the *King's Arms Inn* applied to the railway company to issue tickets for members of a fishing club which met there; trains stopped by request, the waving of a red flag. Rye House became a station in 1846, but it was not until 1849 that platforms and a booking office were built.

Henry Teale leased the Rye House estate in 1849 and set about turning it into a tourist attraction. He made gardens and embellished walkways with statuary; there was a maze and an 'oracle', a sports field and the river for fishing and boating; and the old malt-house was converted into a hall, decorated with banners and armour, for banquets and dinners. In about 1850 Teale bought the inn, which had been called the *King's Arms* since at least 1756, and renamed

103   Detail from Ordnance Survey map, 1898, 6 in., xxxvii NW, showing Hoddesdon, Rye Park and Hailey.

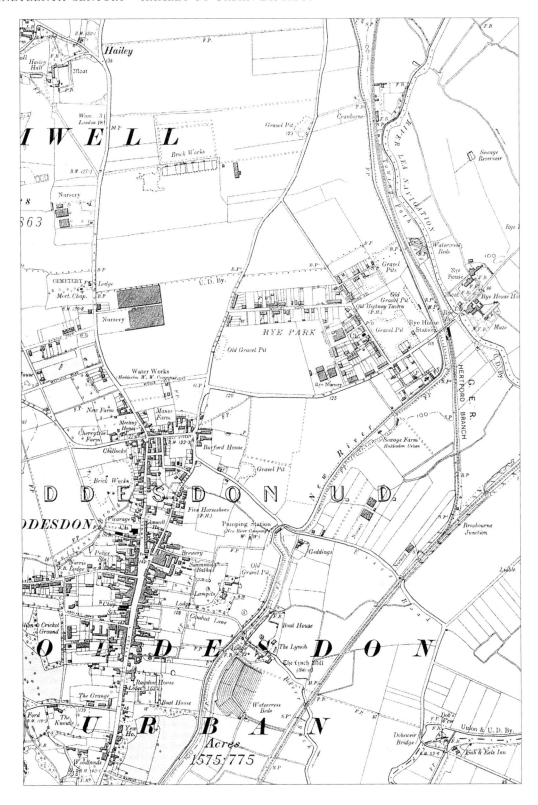

104   Gardens and statuary at the rear of Rye House gatehouse, c.1910.

106   Rye House Hotel.

105   Leaflet advertising Rye House; Great Eastern Railways offered a fare of 1s. 6d. from Bishopsgate to Rye House and back on Saturdays, Sundays and Mondays.

it the *Rye House Hotel*. The double-storey cast-iron window frames which he installed in 1870 came from a house in Cheshunt. A building between the moat and the road housed the Great Bed of Ware, which Teale bought from the *Saracens Head* in Ware in 1870. His venture was highly successful and in 1864 he bought the freehold of the estate. In 1865 Rye House was said to be the principal excursion station on the Great Eastern Railway. Henry Teale died in 1876, aged seventy. His family continued to run the estate until 1904.

IX

Nineteenth Century – People and Places

Nineteenth-century Hoddesdon was home to many different people, some of whose stories have been touched on in the previous chapter, whose lives made an impact on the town and the wider world.

The association of John Warner with Hoddesdon dated from the beginning of the century when in 1802 he married Esther (or Hester) Borham. Esther was the daughter of Thomas Borham, a mealman, who was descended from the one of the earliest Quaker families in Hoddesdon. The family lived at Borham House, which was situated just north of Lowewood. Members of the Warner family, who were also Quakers, had lived in the Waltham Cross, Waltham Abbey and Cheshunt area for many years. An earlier John, the first to be apprenticed to a metal worker in London, had married Sarah Parham of Hoddesdon in 1715. His cousin's son, Tomson Warner, was a brass founder and he established the Crescent Foundries at Fore Street, Cripplegate in London. Tomson's son, John (1776-1852) of Hoddesdon, was apprenticed to the firm and became a Freeman of the Worshipful Company of Founders in 1798.

John and Esther Warner lived in London. In 1807, when Esther was expecting their fourth child, she was tragically murdered whilst visiting her parents in Hoddesdon. Mr and Mrs Borham had recently dismissed one of their servants, Thomas Simmons. He had courted Elizabeth Harris, the Borhams' maid, and asked her to marry him. Mrs Borham had disapproved of the liaison because of Simmons' violent temper, and Elizabeth Harris refused his proposal. Simmons had remained in the town after his dismissal, finding work at Christie's brewery. On the night of 20 October he returned to Borham House threatening murder. Mr and Mrs Borham were at home with their three unmarried daughters, Esther Warner and Mrs Hummerstone, housekeeper of the *Black Lion Inn*. Simmons stabbed Esther Warner and Mrs Hummerstone, who died of their injuries; he also stabbed Mrs Borham, though not fatally, cut Elizabeth Harris's hand as she tried to ward him off

107 *Lowewood (left) and Borham House, 1964.*

and knocked down Mr Borham. Elizabeth managed
to raise the alarm and Simmons was caught nearby.
He was held overnight at the *Bell Inn* before being
transferred to Hertford Gaol.

Simmons was tried for the murder of Sarah
Hummerstone only; Esther Warner's family, being
Quakers, would not testify against him. He was
convicted on 4 March 1808, and executed by hanging
on 7 March, watched by a large crowd. Four years
after the tragedy John Warner married Esther's sister,
Sarah. They were married for 40 years and had 11
children. When his father died, in 1816, John
inherited the brass-founding business, which, as 'John
Warner & Sons', he expanded during the following
years to include the manufacture of church bells. In
1857 the company cast the bells of Big Ben. John
Warner became master of the Founders' Company
in 1834.

In the 1830s Warner built his house, 'Woodlands', at Bradshaws in Hoddesdon. The gardens
were laid out by James Pulham, with cascades, fount-
ains and pools (using pipes and plumbing from the
foundry). Pulham, a plasterer and cement worker,
came to Hoddesdon in 1820, and established a building firm in Amwell Street. He moved to Broxbourne
in 1846 and began to manufacture terracotta. The

108   John Warner, c.1850.

company of Pulham & Son gained a wide reputation
as garden craftsmen and rockery specialists. John
Warner also built the gatehouses known as Gothic
Cottages at Spitalbrook, apparently originally
intending to build on the sloping ground behind
them.

John Warner's interest in gardening led him and
his sons to found the Hoddesdon,
Amwell and Broxbourne Cottage Garden Society in 1842. The gardens at
Woodlands were well stocked, and he
built an orangery to house the more
exotic species. Amongst these were
orchids collected by William Ellis of
Rosehill. The Woodlands gardener, Ben-
jamin Williams, took a great interest in
the cultivation of orchids, and wrote the
Orchid Growers' Manual in collaboration
with Ellis. Williams eventually left Hoddesdon to run his own nursery speciali-
sing in orchids and other exotic plants.

John Warner bought Rawdon House
in 1840 and it remained in the family
until 1866, when it was sold to Charles

109   Woodlands, c.1880.

Battin. The Boys' British School was built in 1841 by John Warner in a field adjacent to the house. He also took an interest in the problems of the poor nationally, and published pamphlets in 1832 and 1845. Rawdon House was rented in 1845 to Mrs. Ellis, who ran her girls' school there. Warner died in 1852, and his wife, Sarah, in 1862. Woodlands descended to Charles Borham Warner. After his death, in 1869, it became the home of the Snow family.

In 1835 John Warner had bought Lowewood with his eldest son, John. John Junior does not seem to have lived there immediately; he and his wife are entered at Woodlands on the 1841 census. John Junior died in 1845, and his widow and two children lived at Lowewood until the early 1860s. By 1865 the house was unoccupied, and was conveyed to John Junior's three spinster half-sisters in that year. Harriette and Celia died before the turn of the century, but Mary lived on at Lowewood until her death in 1921.

Another of John and Sarah's sons, Septimus Warner, built the Italian Cottage, later known as the Spinning Wheel when it became a road-house for

110   The Italian Cottage, 1898; its builder, Septimus Warner, died in 1911, and it later became a road-house called the Spinning Wheel, popular with cyclists.

111   The Coffee Tavern, c.1905, showing (inset) the air vents which are still visible in the side wall.

cyclists. The Coffee Tavern was built in 1883 by members of the Warner family on land offered at a low price by Robert Barclay. Its aim was to encourage temperance by offering non-alcoholic drinks, along with inexpensive food. Tokens worth 2d. were offered to entice people inside.

William Ellis and his second wife, Sarah Stickney Ellis, both made an impact on the life of the town. William Ellis (1794-1872) worked as a gardener before joining the London Missionary Society in 1814. In 1816 he and his first wife, Mary, set sail for the Society Islands. Ellis was an intelligent and energetic man who had studied widely before leaving England. On his arrival he quickly became fluent in the native language and set about translating and printing religious works. In 1822 the Ellis family, now with four children, moved to Hawaii. But Mrs Ellis's health was deteriorating and they returned home via America in 1825. Ellis hoped to return to missionary work, but abandoned the idea when his wife's health did not improve and took the post of Foreign Secretary of the London Missionary Society. Mary Ellis died in 1835.

William Ellis and Sarah Stickney married in 1837. He became ill in 1839 and was recommended to take a year's rest. While travelling in the south of France, they met Mr and Mrs Warner, who described Hoddesdon in glowing terms to them. In 1841 they returned to England and, as William had not completely recovered, he resigned his post and they looked for a house outside London. They remembered the Warners' enthusiasm for Hoddesdon and took a lease on Rosehill in Lord Street. Built about 1790, Rosehill had been the home of the four Misses Kempe in 1800.

Ellis became pastor of the Independent Chapel in 1846. The chapel had been on the Ware Road at Fourways from 1781, but Ellis set about fund-raising for the building of a new church. The Independents of Hoddesdon joined the Congregational Union in 1847 and their new church, built on the site of the *George Inn*, opened in April of that year. The Ellis family took an interest in the British Schools: William

112   William Ellis as an elderly man.

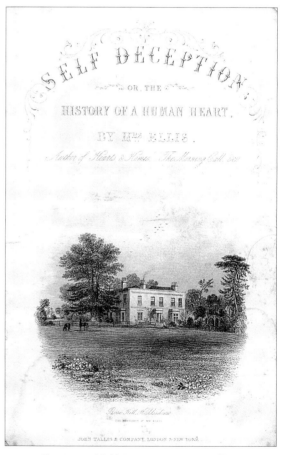

113   Frontispiece of Self Deception *by Sarah Ellis, published 1851, showing Rosehill, the home of William and Sarah Ellis. Local Studies File (Hoddesdon Library)*

114 Sarah Stickney Ellis, a signed portrait from one of her books. Local Studies File (Hoddesdon Library)

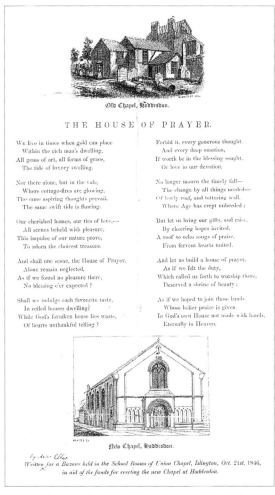

THE HOUSE OF PRAYER.

We live in times when gold can place
  Within the rich man's dwelling,
All gems of art, all forms of grace,
  The tide of luxury swelling.

Nor there alone, but in the vale,
  Where cottage-fires are glowing,
The same aspiring thoughts prevail,
  The same swift tide is flowing.

Our cherished homes, our ties of love,—
  All scenes beheld with pleasure,
This impulse of our nature prove,
  To adorn the choicest treasure.

And shall one scene, the House of Prayer,
  Alone remain neglected,
As if we found no pleasure there,
  No blessing e'er expected ?

Shall we indulge each favourite taste,
  In ceiled houses dwelling?
While God's forsaken house lies waste,
  Of hearts unthankful telling ?

Forbid it, every generous thought,
  And every deep emotion,
If worth be in the blessing sought,
  Or love in our devotion.

No longer mourn the timely fall—
  The change by all things needed—
Of lovely roof, and tottering wall,
  Where Age has crept unheeded ;

But let us bring our gifts, and raise,
  By cheering hopes invited,
A roof to echo songs of praise,
  From fervent hearts united.

And let us build a house of prayer,
  As if we felt the duty,
Which called us forth to worship there,
  Deserved a shrine of beauty ;

As if we hoped to join those bands
  Whose holier praise is given,
In God's own House not made with hands,
  Eternally in Heaven.

by Mrs Ellis
Written for a Bazaar held in the School Rooms of Union Chapel, Islington, Oct. 21st, 1846,
in aid of the funds for erecting the new Chapel at Hoddesdon.

115 Verses by Mrs Ellis, 1846, written to sell in aid of funds for the new Independent Chapel (the Congregational Church) in Hoddesdon. The old chapel at Fourways is shown at the top and the new chapel at the bottom.

Ellis was on the committee of the boys' school, and Sarah and one of her step-daughters, Annie, were on the committee of the girls' and infants' school.

William spent much of the period between 1853 and 1865 doing missionary work in Madagascar, where he found time to collect exotic plants to bring back to England. He presented specimens to Kew Gardens and to the Horticultural Society, and cultivated others at Rosehill. After 1865 he spent much time writing and giving lectures, and was active until a few days before his death in 1872.

Sarah Stickney (1799-1872) was a published author before she met William Ellis. Her novels had a strong moral theme, and she wrote a series of well-received 'Conduct' books, of which *The Women of England, their Social Duties and Domestic Habits* was the first to be published in 1838. The books advocated moral training for young ladies, development of character, and practical preparation for running a household, stressing the importance of a woman's place in life as a helper and companion of her menfolk. These sentiments, it was reportedly said at the time, accounted for their popularity because men found them very suitable presents for their wives and daughters.

Mrs Ellis felt that the schools available for wealthy middle-class girls put too much emphasis on the 'genteel' pursuits of music, sketching, embroidery and deportment. She wanted to put the ideas embodied in the 'Conduct' books into practice, and in 1845 she leased Rawdon House from John Warner and opened a school there. The school was successful, but attracted some adverse comment. Some men, far from applauding her ideas, thought that she was encouraging women to 'manage' men, and the school, disguised as Capsicum House, was lampooned in a series of articles in *Punch* in 1847. Sarah Ellis was not a radical; she wanted to improve girls' education within the framework of current society, and so she

116　Rawdon House, a print made for William and Sarah Ellis.

CAPSICUM HOUSE FOR YOUNG LADIES.

CHAPTER I.

A VISIT TO CAPSICUM HOUSE. MISS GRIFFIN ON THE FIRST
PRINCIPLES OF STUFFING.

E shall never for-
get the emotion
that softly broke
within us on our
first visit to Cap-
sicum House. We
know not how it
is, but we have
always felt a par-
ticular respect for
Boarding Schools
for Young Ladies.
We are open to
allow the oddity
of the taste; we
confess to the ec-
centricity — but
so it is. We have
a knack of look-
ing upon such
abiding-places as
great manufac-
tories of the do-
mestic virtues—
as the salt-cellars
of a vain and fool-
ish world. And now we are prone to consider them as towers and
castles—we of course speak of Schools Finishing—whence, as in the
precious old times, young ladies walk forth, their accomplishments
breaking like sunbeams about them, to bless, elevate, and purify
ungrateful, wayward, earthy man. As MISS GRIFFIN herself was
wont to say, sometimes with little tears glistening like pins'-heads
in her eyes—as that great woman was accustomed to observe of her
own pupils—"Dear little things! they are made too good for men;
but then—poor souls! it's their mission." ·

also irritated some of the more free-thinking women authors of her time. However, she probably gave her pupils a better learning experience than many other girls had at that time. When Rawdon House was sold, in 1865, the school was transferred to Finchley, run by the last of Mrs Ellis's partners, Miss Taylor. Sarah Stickney Ellis died in 1872, a few days after her husband. She is buried in the Quaker burial ground in Hoddesdon.

Rawdon House was bought by Henry Ricardo in 1875, and he employed Ernest George and Harold Peto to build the north wing. George became one of the leading country house architects of his day. In 1892 C.P. Christie became the owner, and in 1898 Miss White bought the property and gave it to the nuns of the Order of St Augustine. From then until 1969 it was known as St Monica's Priory.

Robert Barclay was another bene-factor of Hoddesdon. He settled in the town in 1871. The site he bought and renamed High Leigh had previously been High Wyches (1535) and then High Grounds (1677). In 1851 Charles Webb, a gold lace manufacturer, owned the site and built the centre part of the present house. He also altered the line of Lord Street to take it further from the house. Robert Barclay enlarged the house and built the lodge in Cock Lane, approached by a bridge built by Pulham & Son. He planted Beech Walk and the plane trees in Park View, landscaped Lowfield, and

117　A cartoon from Punch, *1847, lampooning the school at Rawdon House as Capsicum House. By permission of the British Library (Shelf mark, LD34a)*

118   High Leigh, c.1900.

made the lake, which is fed by Spital Brook. Robert Barclay offered the use of the part of Lowfield near Park View for a cricket field and a football pitch for the people of Hoddesdon. He was a churchwarden at Hoddesdon church and took an interest in the development of the church at Rye Park. In 1893 he became High Sheriff of Hertfordshire.

119   The Lodge in Cock Lane has Robert Barclay's initials and the date 1895 on the front wall. The bridge over Spitalbrook was built by Pulham and Son.

Yew House was only given that name in 1800, from a yew tree which stood by the house. The tree remained until 1890. The house itself was much altered early in the 19th century. From about 1790 it was the home of Edward Christian, brother of Fletcher Christian who led the mutiny on the *Bounty*. Edward Christian held the post of Professor of Law at Downing College, Cambridge and was amongst the first members of staff of the East India College, Haileybury, when it opened in 1806. He was still resident in the area, and acting as a Hertfordshire magistrate, in 1822. He died in 1823, but whether he died at Hoddesdon or at Downing College, Cambridge seems uncertain. There is a memorial tablet to him in Broxbourne church.

Admiral William Peere Williams owned Yew House from about 1803. In 1809 a vestry minute noted that he had given permission for the girls of the Sunday school to use the chancel seats in Broxbourne church which had been adopted for the use of Yew

120 *Yew House, left, and its stable block, right, 1898.*

House in 1770. Williams had been made an Admiral in 1801, and was promoted to the rank of High Admiral of the Fleet in 1831. He died in 1832 at Hoddesdon, aged 91, and is buried in the family vault at Broxbourne.

Yew House was bought in 1836 by Miss Walmsley, and later occupied by Donat Henchy O'Brien, whose wife was Miss Walmsley's niece. O'Brien was born in 1785, joined the navy at the age of 11, and had been involved in active service by the time he was fourteen. He served throughout the Napoleonic Wars, and published accounts in 1814 and 1839 of his experiences of war which included shipwreck, captivity in a French prisoner-of-war camp and eventual escape to fight again. He retired from active service in 1821, but was promoted to the rank of Rear Admiral in 1852. While living in Yew House he often walked down the lane to the south of the house and on to the marshes, and the lane became known locally as 'the admiral's walk'. When houses were built on the marshes in 1880 the lane was made into a

121 *Donat Henchy O'Brien.*

road and called Admirals Walk. Admiral O'Brien died in 1852 and is buried in Broxbourne church.

In 1836 Dr William Gosse took on the practice at Rathmore House. He and his wife Agnes had seven children, all born in Hoddesdon. The eldest child, Agnes, wrote memoirs in 1905 which contain recollections of her childhood. She described the Hoddesdon of the 1840s as 'a small and highly select town' with 'an air about it of intense, uncompromising respectability' and 'its inhabitants, of the upper class, consisted chiefly of old ladies with small means and large ideas'. The Gosse family left Hoddesdon in 1850 to emigrate to the new province of South Australia. One of the Gosse children, William Christie Gosse (his middle name taken from the brewing family of Christies), became a land surveyor. In 1873 W.C. Gosse was chosen to lead an expedition to find a way west from Alice Springs to the coast. During his expedition he sighted the great red rock, Uluru, and became the first European to visit and climb it. Unaware of its significance to the indigenous people, he named it Ayers Rock, after the Premier of South Australia, Sir Henry Ayers. Although Gosse was unable to complete his journey to the coast because of lack of water, the information about the terrain he brought back and the maps he made enabled another explorer, John Forrest, to find a way through to the west coast the following year. William Christie Gosse (1842-81) is commemorated on an Australian postage stamp issued in 1976.

The rising population of Hoddesdon meant there was an opening for another doctor apart from

122   Eighteen-cent Australian stamp, 1976, depicting W.C. Gosse. © Australia Post. National Philatelic Collection, Australia Post.

the Rathmore House practice. Dr William Horley was registrar for births, deaths and marriages in 1834, and was living in the High Street in 1839. Later he lived and worked at Stanboroughs, followed in the practice by his son, W.L. Horley. Between about 1860 and 1890 part of Stanboroughs was used as a school for servants called 'The Training or Industrial House for Servants'. The establishment was run by a Mrs Draper under the auspices of various local ladies

123   The High Street, looking north, c.1900. Stanboroughs is on the extreme right.

124   Norris Lodge and Dr Bisdee, 1897.

century, when it was the home o
Colonel Rawlins. Rawlins tried and
failed to enter parliament in 1806
The Reverend Jones wrote in hi
diary that Rawlins borrowed £3(
from him for his campaign, whick
he was very reluctant to repay.

Montague House was the home
of John Loudon McAdam, the road
building pioneer, from 1827 unti
1836. His method was to make a
roadbed about 10 in. deep of smal
stones, which would be compacted
by passing traffic to provide a
smooth waterproof surface. George
Allen, who made tools to McAdam'
designs for road repair, also lived in
Hoddesdon at this time. McAdan

including Miss Faithfull, daughter of Mrs Faithfull
of the Grange School.

Dr Bisdee joined Dr Horley in 1878, and in
1895 he moved to Norris Lodge in Lord Street,
where he carried on his practice until his retirement
in 1908. Norris Lodge had been known as Broxbourne Lodge or Cucumber Hall earlier in the 19th

was appointed Surveyor General of roads in 1827
and he and his sons worked with various Turnpike
Trusts. There was a toll-gate at Spitalbrook, which in
1840 was moved further up the hill, and later moved
back down. The turnpike system was abolished in
1872, the gate was removed and the toll-house was
sold. McAdam died not in Hoddesdon, but on a visi

125   Montague House (centre), 1861, home of J.L. McAdam from 1827 until 1836.

126   The rear of the Grange, 1988.

127   Bricks of the Grange gate pier inscribed with the name of A. Chittenden and the date April 1876.

to his native Scotland in 1836. There is a memorial tablet to him in Broxbourne church.

The Grange was sold by the Hughes family to Robert Warner in 1854, and was let to Mrs Faithfull, widow of the rector of Hatfield. With her son-in-law, the Reverend Chittenden, she ran a boys' preparatory school there. The pupils made full use of the soft stone of the gateposts to leave their marks for posterity. Among the many carved names is 'A Chittenden' (Arthur, the headmaster's son), and it is said that another pupil, A.J. Balfour, who became Prime Minister in 1902, also inscribed his initials here. After Mrs Faithfull's death, in 1865, the Reverend Chittenden became the proprietor, and the school continued at the Grange until 1905. Ownership of the house passed to Robert Barclay in 1872.

Burford House was owned by Mrs Whittingstall, widow of the brewery owner, until 1830. It was then bought by E. Waller of Broxbourne Mill, who gave it its name. After Waller's death in 1840, Burford House became a school run by Warner Tuck. In 1845 the Agricultural and Scientific School was established at Burford House by W. Haselwood. The school was well sited as regards agriculture. The area from Cheshunt through Hoddesdon to Ware was considered to be a 'noble vein of land' by Arthur

Young, Secretary to the Board of Agriculture, in his report of 1804, and he judged the valley to have the best land in Hertfordshire. The scientific side of the school included geology. One of its pupils, Edward Hargraves, combined practical skills gained in the Californian gold rush with a spell of tuition at Burford House to predict the localities of gold fields in Australia. He was so successful that he was appointed Commissioner of Crown Lands in New South Wales and given a government reward of £10,000.

The Burford House school seems to have broadened its curriculum through the years. By 1850 it was the Agricultural, General, Practical and Scientific School, employing a French and German master as well as Mr Haselwood and two other masters. It was subsequently the Scientific and Commercial School and by 1860 was the 'Grammar School'. In its early days the school took adult students (Hargraves was in his 30s when he studied there in 1851), but latterly its aim was to prepare boys for a college education. By 1882, after Haselwood's time, it had assumed the mantle of the Queen Elizabeth Grammar School of 1560 and made the claim that the Marquess of Salisbury had the right to nominate a boy for a scholarship worth £10 a year to St John's College, Cambridge from either

128 *(top)*   *Burford House Academy, 1870.*

129 *(above)*   *The building which housed the Middle Class Academy.*

130 *(right)*   *Terms and conditions of the Middle Class Academy in the 1880s.*

Select Middle Class Academy,

HIGH STREET,

HODDESDON.

Miss M. H. ASHFORD, in returning thanks for the patronage she has received, begs to assure her kind supporters that she continues to conduct the above Academy, and trusts by strict attention to the duties devolving on her, to merit a continuance of their favours.

Term commences .... *188 .*

Terms per Quarter.

	s.	d.
Instruction in English with Plain and Fancy Needlework	12	6
Pupils under 8 years of age	10	6
Music	12	6
French	10	6
Singing (by a master)	2	6
Drawing—Freehand and Model (by a master)	3	6

N.B. Private pupils received for the Singing and Drawing Classes.

this school or Westminster. Despite this initiative, the school was without masters by 1886. The vice-principal, Reverend H. Pretyman Waller, became head of St Catherine's School, a preparatory boys' school, on the St Catherine's estate, which from about 1883 was being built south of Spitalbrook.

There were a number of private schools in and around Hoddesdon in the 19th century. Many were short lived, but one which ran from the latter years of the 19th century into the 20th century was the Middle Class Academy, near the Grange. When Burford House ceased to be a school Thomas Murray Gardiner established a business manufacturing cricket bats and tennis rackets there. He also ran an ironmonger's in the High Street, at the rear of which bicycles were made until the late 1920s.

Harriet Auber was the author of many hymns and devotional poems. She moved from Broxbourne to Hoddesdon in 1818 and lived at The Rise in Amwell Street. Her most famous hymn 'Our blest Redeemer ere He breathed', written in 1829, is said to have been scratched on a pane of glass in her house, because she did not want to risk forgetting the newly-composed lines while she looked for pen and paper. Although the pane of glass, reportedly last seen in 1875, disappeared, the hymn survives. Harriet Auber died in 1862 and is buried on the west side of St Catherine and St Paul's church; there is a memorial to her in the east window of the church.

131 Harriet Auber (1773-1862), and the inscriptions in the east window of St Catherine and St Paul's church which commemorate her. Her forename is given as Henriette in this memorial window.

X

1900-1974 – Urban District to Borough

During the 20th century the growth of the town continued and many new housing estates and industrial areas were built. The Urban District was enlarged and in 1974 the Borough of Broxbourne was formed. The brewery continued to be a major employer in Hoddesdon in the early years of the century, but suffered a series of setbacks. A fire in 1905 caused over £10,000 of damage and later a yeast infection in the beer affected production. After the death of Captain John Fairfax Christie the brewery was sold.

Captain Christie had been badly injured in the First World War and committed suicide in 1927. The brewery was first offered to McMullens who refused it, but the Cannon Brewery of Clerkenwell acquired the brewery, Rye House and 159 pubs in a deal finalised in 1928. The brewery was closed, some of its buildings were demolished and others were modified for other uses.

A purpose-built cinema was opened in Burford Street in 1913. This operated until 1930 when its

132   Christie's Brewery, c.1920.

10   *Hoddesdon & District Infant Welfare Building Fund Fete and Pageant*

BEFORE YOU GO HOME
BE SURE TO
Visit Ye Olde
Rye House Hostlerie

THE HOME OF RUMBOLD *and*
ISAAC WALTON'S HOUSE OF CALL

In these Romantic Surroundings you may obtain

Christie's
FAMOUS
ALES & STOUTS
Brewed at
HODDESDON

Also WINES, SPIRITS, MINERALS and
Refreshment generally

WHAT A CHARMING SETTING IN WHICH TO REFRESH
ONESELF AT THE END OF A PERFECT DAY!!!

The Cinema, Burford St., HODDESDON.
For Three Days Only.
Monday, February 2nd, to Wednesday, February 4th, 1914.

The Battle of Gettysburg.

The Crucial Contest in the American Civil War.

Fought on Wednesday, Thursday and Friday, July 1st, 2nd & 3rd, 1863,
at Gettysburg, Pennsylvania, a rural village of 3,000 inhabitants; the
focus of a well cultivated but rugged and heavily wooded area.

Scene from "The Battle of Gettysburg."

THE CHARACTERS

LAMAR	Editor of "The Gazette."
JACK LAMAR	His Son and Assistant.
DR. BURK	Their Neighbour.
VIRGINIA BURK	Dr. Burk's Daughter.
JIM BURK	His Son and Jack's Friend.
MAJOR POLLARD, A Southern Gentleman and Officer in the Confederate Army.	

133   *Advertisement for Christie's beer, Rye House, 1924.*   **134**   *Leaflet for the cinema, Burford Street, 1914.*

135   *The Pavilion cinema and the brewery buildings in the 1960s.*

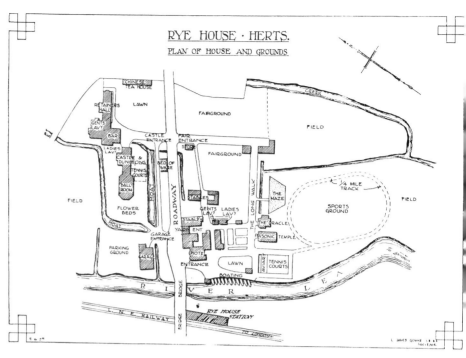

RYE HOUSE · HERTS.
PLAN OF HOUSE AND GROUNDS

136   Plan of Rye House grounds, c.1925.

137   Rye House, rear.

owners, Shipman and King, opened the larger Pavilion Cinema which had over 800 seats. The old cinema became the Robert Gilling Hall in 1949, headquarters of the Haileybury Boys Club. The building housing the Pavilion was part of the former Christie brewery complex. The cinema ran until 1972, when it was converted to a Bingo club. The Civic Hall, a multi-purpose building, catering for many functions including cinema, opened in 1976.

Rye House had been bought in 1904 by Christies and continued to operate for some years after the sale of the brewery. It was still popular enough in the 1920s for the last police horse in Hertfordshire to be employed in Hoddesdon for crowd control purposes. On occasions PC Oliver and his horse 'Benny Ally' were called on to clear the ballroom of intoxicated customers. The crowds from London were not always popular with the locals, who dubbed them the 'rent dodgers', considering that their day's outing might well be designed to evade the rent

138 *St Cuthbert's church, Whitley Road, 1960.*

collector. Rye House was damaged by fire shortly before the Second World War. The old ballroom, situated at the rear of the gatehouse, was used as a roller-skating rink for some years and the lower floor of the gatehouse itself was the men's toilet. By 1951 a visitor noted that, although a wooden arch advertised a skating rink, the rink itself was 'quite invisible'. The gatehouse continued to deteriorate until 1970 when it was bought and restored by the Lee Valley Regional Park.

St Cuthbert's church in Rye Park was built in 1908, but it was not until the 1920s that the area became more built up. In 1921 council houses were built in Rye Road. New roads were developed north and south of Rye Road and to the west of Stanstead Road.

The 1920s witnessed several improvements in services and utilities. Hoddesdon's bus service had consisted of a horse-bus which plied the route from Broxbourne station to the town centre until 1921,

when the first motor bus service ran through the town. However, in the early years of the century road accidents were not uncommon. In 1913 a road accident occurred at Hailey when a motor bus taking workers on a firm's outing crashed, killing five people.

The gas lighting in the streets of Hoddesdon was superseded by electric lighting in 1923. The gas works near the railway was absorbed by the Tottenham Gas Company in 1932; in 1951, Rye House Power Station started to generate electricity. In 1922 the Urban District Council bought the market rights from the Marquess of Salisbury. The market continued to deal in livestock until about 1930, after which it became a general market. The remaining livestock sales, mainly of poultry, moved to an area behind the *Salisbury Arms*.

Hoddesdon increased greatly in size during the 20th century. The houses of Yewlands estate were built on the land round Yew House in 1904. The Forres estate, advertised as Hoddesdon's garden

139   Workmen from Hamilton's Nursery, Waltham Cross, 1913. The bus was involved in an accident near Hailey Lane as they returned from their outing, killing five of the men.

suburb, was built in the late 1930s and was followed in the post-war period by many other housing estates.

The two world wars took their toll on Hoddesdon more in the count of young lives lost in the fighting than in damage to the town. The war memorial was erected in 1921, and 40 extra names were added in 1951. There was no civilian loss of life in Hoddesdon in the First World War, but in the Second a line of 14 bombs fell between Ware Road and Cock Lane in 1941, killing two people. Nissen huts, the multi-purpose semi-cylindrical buildings made of corrugated iron and originally used for military purposes in the First World War, were manufactured near Rye House. Rosehill was used as a V.A.D. Hospital during the First World War. From 1926 until just before its demolition in 1955 it was the home of Joseph Gurney Barclay and his family.

Lowewood housed Hoddesdon's public library from 1937 until 1977. It had belonged to members of the Warner family for 100 years. When Mary Warner died, in 1921, her niece, Elizabeth Ann

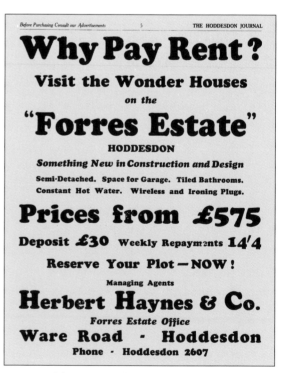

140   Advertisement for houses on the Forres estate, 1936.

Warner, owned the house until her death in 1936. Lowewood was bought by Douglas Taylor, who gave it to the town to be used as a library and museum in memory of his wife. The library was open two afternoons and two evenings a week, with E.W. Paddick as assistant librarian. In 1942 he was appointed as full-time librarian, and in 1946 Charles S. Whitley entrusted the family's collection of antiquities to Paddick for display at Lowewood. Some of the collection had previously been on display at the Clock House and some had been kept by the family. The Whitley collection was displayed alongside records of the Urban District Council in the 'Records Room' at Lowewood. Following donations from the public, the council took responsibilty

141   Gardiner's ironmongery advertisement, 1939.

142 (below left)   Front of Hoddesdon Journal, *with Nissen hut cartoon, 1939.*

143 (below right)   Poster announcing the opening of the Public Library at Lowewood, 1937.

for the display in 1949 and Paddick became curator. In 1960 he formally handed over his collection of records to the museum. Paddick retired as librarian in 1963, but remained curator until 1974, two years before he died.

The library moved to new, bigger premises in the town centre in 1977. It was decided that Lowewood should house the museum and the Broxbourne Arts Council. The museum collection from Cheshunt library was added to the Lowewood collection, to form a museum for the whole Borough of Broxbourne. The museum, occupying the upper rooms of Lowewood, was opened to the public in 1982. The Samaritan Woman statue, which had been deemed unrepairable in 1894, was restored by Charles Giddings, and was re-erected behind the Council offices in 1937. In 1987 the statue was moved to the garden of Lowewood. Charles Giddings also sculpted busts of George VI, George V, and Edward VII which adorned the pediments of the Clock House.

Early in the 20th century Hoddesdon's church was dedicated to St Paul. In 1901 a peal of eight bells was donated by the Christie family in memory of Charles Peter Christie and his wife, Isabel. It was at the ceremony to dedicate these and the bell tower that the church officially became St Paul's. The street name, Pauls Lane, predates the church name and may have influenced the choice of saint. In 1976 the church was re-dedicated to both St Paul and St Catherine.

Robert Barclay died in 1921. High Leigh was sold to 'The First Conference Estate Ltd', which provides conference facilities for Christian organisations. Barclay Park was given to the town by the Barclay family, the portion between the lake and Beech Walk by Deed of Gift in 1935, and the remainder as far as Cock Lane in 1936.

A new school, Burford Street Senior County Council School, opened in Hoddesdon in 1930. This took senior pupils from the Boys' National School,

144   *Charles Giddings with the Samaritan Woman statue.*

145   *The Clock House, 1962.*

146   Hoddesdon parish church, early 20th century.

147   High Leigh Conference Centre.

148   Barclay Park lake, 1973.

149   Beech Walk, 1962.

the Girls' National School and the Girls' British School. In 1948 the school became the Hoddesdon Secondary School, and moved in 1953 to new premises in Stanstead Road. In 1968, with the advent of comprehensive education, the school was renamed the John Warner School. When the seniors moved to Stanstead Road the premises became a junior school, renamed Haslewood School. The infants remained at the school in Pauls Lane until 1971, when they relocated to a new school on the Haslewood site. The school buildings nearest to the entrance to Pauls Lane were demolished to allow for road widening.

As the town grew, more infant and junior schools were built to cater for younger children and Sheredes Comprehensive School was built in 1969 for senior pupils. Hailey Hall School was built in the 1960s on the site of the old manor house of Hailey.

Many of the older houses in the town have either been demolished or converted for other uses. Yew

150   National School buildings, 1972.

House was used as a girls' school from 1929, run by the Misses Quibell. After the Second World War it was left unoccupied until 1962, when it was demolished. Cedar Green now stands on the site. Stanboroughs was bought in 1901 by Dr Wells, who was a medical practitioner in Hoddesdon for many years, finally retiring in 1947. He rented Stanboroughs to the Conservative and Unionist Club, of which he was a founder member. Norris Lodge was the home of the Gardner family from 1909. Celia Davies, née Gardner, was seven when the family moved in, and later wrote about her childhood in Hoddesdon in her book *Clean Clothes on Sunday*. The house was demolished in the 1930s; houses were built on the road frontage, but a strip of what had been the garden around Woollens Brook remained open.

Rawdon House was St Monica's Priory until 1969. Although threatened with demolition, the house survived, used as offices. Esdale House was demolished in 1961 and the Roman Catholic Church

of St Augustine's was built on the site. The last private owners of the Grange were the Tuke Taylors. After Mrs Tuke Taylor's death in 1968, the Grange was bought for conversion to homes for the elderly. The land of the Grange and of Rawdon House was sold

151   Rawdon House sale document, c.1970.

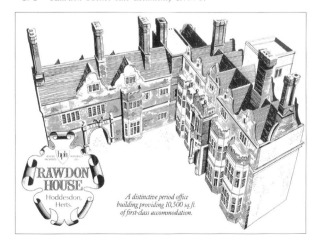

for housing. Woodlands was owned by J.A. Hillyer from 1919 until 1938. After his death the ground floor was used by Hoddesdon Urban District Council and the first floor was made into flats. The building was demolished in 1967 to make way for a new police station. The stables and the orangery of Woodlands were converted to private dwellings in the late 1950s and the Gothic Cottages were demolished in the early 1960s. Borham House was demolished in 1965, and a new Health Centre was built which opened in 1969.

Hoddesdonbury was owned by the actress, Lady Maud Tree (1864-1937), during the later years of her life. In 1948 it became the home of Admiral Sir Alexander and Lady Juliet Bingley. Admiral Bingley (1905-72) commanded various ships during the Second World War and sent the message reporting the sinking of the *Bismarck*. In the post-war years he was 5th Sea Lord, Commander-in-Chief, Mediterranean, and Commander-in-Chief, Portsmouth. After his retirement he was Rear Admiral of the United Kingdom from 1966-8.

The town centre underwent great changes in the 1960s. In 1964 the *Bull Inn* was demolished. In the same year the area to the north of the Clock House, including the *Maidenhead Inn*, was cleared in preparation for building the Tower Centre, which opened in 1967. The buildings around the Clock House were removed, leaving just the Clock Tower. Another shopping precinct was made when the Congregational Church and other buildings were demolished in 1967 to make way for the Fawkon Walk development.

Major road reorganisation took place in the 1970s. The bypass to the west of the town opened in 1974. The houses on the western side of Amwell Street beyond Woollens Brook, Fourways House and the *Duke William of Cumberland* were demolished in 1974 to allow for road widening. In 1975, the Dinant Relief Road and Charlton Way, to the east of the town, were built, and Conduit Lane was widened.

152   *The Roman Catholic Church of St Augustine.*

153   *Woodlands, 1964.*

154   *Hoddesdonbury, 1943.*

155   Aerial view of Hoddesdon, looking south-west, c.1960.
156   The High Street, looking north, c.1950s.

157 The Maidenhead *inn, c.1960.*
158 The High Pavement, Amwell Street, c.1960.

159 *Aerial view of Hoddesdon, 1970, looking south-east beyond the newly built Tower Centre to Charlton Way and the Lampits estate. The Lynch and the area where watercress was once grown are in the background.*

160   *The High Street, 1970; the Tower Centre was completed in 1967.*

161   *Fourways, 1967, with Fourways House on the left and the* Duke William of Cumberland *inn on the right.*

162   Crest of the Urban District of Hoddesdon.

163   The council offices, built in 1935.

   The changes in local government which culminated in the formation of the Borough of Broxbourne had begun with the enlargement of the Urban District of Hoddesdon in 1935 to include Broxbourne and Wormley. The district was divided into four wards, Town, Rye Park, Broxbourne and Wormley. A crest was devised: Town was represented by the wheel of St Catherine, Rye Park by Rye House gatehouse, Broxbourne by a badger, and Wormley by a gridirion, the instrument of martyrdom of St Lawrence, to whom Wormley church is dedicated. The crest also featured a tree to denote the importance of the woodlands in past times. In 1947 the wards were revised and the North ward was added, but the crest was not altered.

   The old council offices next to Yew Arbour were no longer used after 1926. Yew Arbour itself was demolished in 1959, and Priory Close was built on the site. Between 1926 and 1935 the council offices were next to Hogges Hall, in what had been the offices of Hunts, the builders. In 1935 purpose-built council offices were built just south of Cock Lane.

   As a result of local government reorganisation the Urban Districts of Hoddesdon and Cheshunt were merged in 1974 to form the Borough of Broxbourne. A new coat of arms was devised incorporating features of the coats of arms of both districts. With the forming of the new borough, a new era began with its story to be told in the future.

Bibliography

The following list represents the main sources of information that I have used. Not listed are the many general reference works (such as biographical dictionaries) or numerous sources which have provided only minor contributions.

Allen, G.A.T., *Christ's Hospital* (1984)

Andrews, H.C., 'Broxbourne; its Churches and their Builders', *Transactions of the East Herts Archaeological Society*, vol.8 (1928-9)

Andrews, H.C., 'Broxbourne; the Say Family', *Transactions of the East Herts Archaeological Society*, vol.9 (1934-6)

Andrews, H.C., 'Sidelights on Brasses in Hertfordshire Churches, XXI. Broxbourne Church', *Transactions of the East Herts Archaeological Society*, vol.11 pt.2 (1941)

Andrews, R.T., 'The Rye House Castle and Manor of Rye', *Transactions of the East Herts Archaeological Society*, vol.2 pt.1 (1902)

Andrews, R.T. and Gerish, W.B., 'The Leper Hospital, Hoddesdon', *Transactions of the East Herts Archaeological Society*, vol.1 pt. 3 (1901)

Armitage, H., *Russell and Rye House* (1948)

Austin, Peter, 'The Leasing of Lord Burghley's Hoddesdon Woodland in 1595, an insight into woodmanship', *Hertfordshire's Past*, pt.41(1996)

Baumer, L.E., *Foundations* (1944)

Branch Johnson, W., *Companion into Hertfordshire* (1952)

Branch Johnson, W., *Hertfordshire Inns* (1962)

Branch Johnson, W., *Industrial Archaeology of Hertfordshire* (1970)

Burnby, J.G.L. and Parker, M., *Navigation of the River Lea (The Edmonton Hundred Historical Society)* (1978)

Cecil, David, *The Cecils of Hatfield House* (1973)

Chauncy, Sir Henry, *The Historical Antiquities of Hertfordshire* (1700)

Christie, O.F., *Diary of William Jones, 1777-1821* (1929)

Clutterbuck, Robert, *The History and Antiquities of the County of Hertford* (1815)

Cussans, John Edwin, *History of Hertfordshire* (1870-81)

Davies, C., *Clean Clothes on Sunday* (1974)

Davies, Robert (ed.), *Life of Marmaduke Rawdon of York (The Camden Society)* (1863)

Dent, David, *Broxbourne and Wormley Past in Pictures* (1995)

Dent, David, *Hoddesdon's Past in Pictures* (1992)

Dent, David, *150 Years of the Hertford and Ware Railway* (1993)

Doggett, N., 'Medieval Hospitals in Hertfordshire', *Hertfordshire's Past*, vol.38 (1995)

Doree, Stephen G. (ed.), *The Parish Register and Tithing Book of Thomas Hassall of Amwell* (1989)

Doree, S.G. and Perman, D., *Amwell and Stanstead Past in Pictures* (1997)

Doubleday, H. Arthur, *Victoria County History of the Counties of England – A History of Hertfordshire* (1902)

Edwards, Jack, *The Victoria Cottage Homes* (1997)

Ellis, John Eimeo, *Life of William Ellis* (1873)

Essex-Lopristi, Michael, *Exploring the New River* (1986)

Evans, Sir John, 'Opening of a Barrow at Broxbournebury', *Transactions of the East Herts Archaeological Society*, vol.2 pt.1 (1902)

Eyles, A. and Skone, K., *The Cinemas of Hertfordshire* (1985)

Friar, S., *Batsford Companion to Local History* (1991)

Gandon, P., *The House of my Pilgrimage* (1976)

Garside, S., *Hoddesdon Highlights* (1988)

Gosse, F., *The Gosses, An Anglo-Australian Family* (1981)

Gosse, W.C., *W.C. Gosse's Explorations, 1873. Report and Diary of Mr W.C. Gosse's Central and Western Exploring Expedition, 1873.* (1874)

Gough, J.W., *Sir Hugh Myddleton* (1964)

Harper, C.G., *Roads* (1905)

Harvey, W.J., *Great Amwell, Past and Present* (1896)

Harvey, John H., *William Worcestre, Itineraries* (1969)

Hay, A.G., *After Glow Memories* (1905)

Hayllar, H.F., *The Chronicles of Hoddesdon* (1948)

Hey, David, *Oxford Companion to Local and Family History* (1996)

Hoare, R.G., *Broxbourne Past and Present* (1897)

Holden, Robert, *Historical Record of the Worcester Regiment* (1887)

Hurt, J.S., *Bringing Literacy to Rural England* (1972)

Joliffe, G. and Jones, A., *Hertfordshire Inns and Public Houses* (1995)

Jones, A. (ed.), *Hertfordshire 1731 – 1800*, as recorded in *The Gentleman's Magazine* (1993)

Jones-Baker, D., *The Folklore of Hertfordshire* (1977)

Jones-Baker, D. (ed.), *Hertfordshire in History* (1991)

Killick, H.F., 'The Memoirs of Sir Marmaduke Rawdon, Kt.', *Yorkshire Archaeological Journal*, vol.25 pt. 99 (1896)

Kiln, Robert, *The Dawn of History in East Herts.* (1986)

Knight, J.D.S., *Then Now & Then What* (1992)

Lempriere, W., *A History of the Girls School of Christ's Hospital* (1924)

Lewis, Jim, *London's Lea Valley: Britain's Best Kept Secret* (1999)

Lewis, Jim, *London's Lea Valley: More Secrets Revealed* (2002)

Matthews, C.M., *Haileybury since Roman Times*, 2nd edn. (2000)

Morris, John (ed.), *Domesday Book 12, Hertfordshire* (1976)

Munby, Lionel, *The Common People are not Nothing* (1995)

Niblett, Rosalind, *Roman Hertfordshire (*1995)

Osborn, N., *The Story of the Hertfordshire Police* (1969)

Paddick, E.W., *Hoddesdon, Tales of a Hertfordshire Town* (1971)

Page, F.M., *Christ's Hospital, Hertford* (1953)

Parker, J., *Nothing for Nothing for Nobody* (1986)

Pereira, H.B., *The Colour of Chivalry* (1951)

Perman, D., *John Scott of Amwell* (2001)

Pevsner, N., *The Buildings of England – Hertfordshire* 2nd edn. (1992)

Poole, Helen, *Here for the Beer – a Gazetteer of the Brewers of Hertfordshire* (1984)

Reader, F.W., 'Some Examples of Tudor and Jacobean Wall Paintings in Herts and Elsewhere', *Transactions of the East Herts Archaeological Society*, vol.11 pt.2 (1941)

Robinson, G., *Barracuda Guide to County History, 3, Hertfordshire* (1978)

Rook, T., *Hertfordshire Histories, Roads* (1991)

Rood, Tony, *A History of Hertfordshire* (1997)

Salmon, N., *The History of Hertfordshire* (1728)

Savage, Anne, *The Anglo-Saxon Chronicles (translation)* (1984)

Sheldrick, G., *The Accounts of Thomas Green* (1992)

Smith, J.T., *English Houses 1200-1800, The Hertfordshire Evidence* (1992)

Starkey, David, 'The String Untuned, a Riot at Hoddesdon, 1534', *History Today*, pt.12 (1979)

Stewart, L.D., *John Scott of Amwell* (1956)

Thomas, I., *Haileybury 1806-1987* (1987)

Thompson, F., *Newport Grammar School, Essex* (1974)

Tomkins, M., *So that was Hertfordshire: Travellers' Jottings, 1322-1887* (1998)

Tregelles, J.A., *A History of Hoddesdon* (1908)

Urwick, W., *Nonconformity in Hertfordshire* (1884)

Walton, Izaak, *The Compleat Angler*, 5th edn., reprint (1897)

Young, Arthur, *General View of the Agriculture of the County of Hertfordshire* (1804)

I have also consulted various sources at the Hertfordshire Archives and Local Studies (HALS) in County Hall, Hertford, the Hoddesdon Local Studies Library and Lowewood Museum, Hoddesdon. These include newspaper and magazine articles, trade directories, local information leaflets, the *Transactions of the East Herts Archaeological Society* and the *Calendar of the Manuscripts of the Most Hon. The Marquess of Salisbury*. Amongst the unpublished sources I have used are The Rawdon Book, The Thorowgood Book, parish records, school minute books, and notes by E.W. Paddick and other local historians. I am also grateful to HALS for providing me with a print-out of relevant items from the Hertfordshire Sites and Monuments Records database.

Index

✧

Page numbers in **bold** type refer to illustrations

Admirals Walk, 84
agriculture, 3, 7, 74, 87
Allen, George, 86
almshouses, 14, 15, 49, 50, 61, 62
Amwell. *See* Great Amwell
Amwell manor, 8, 10, 11
Amwell Street, 52, 64, 66, **72**, 72, 78, 89, 100, **102**
Anglo-Saxon era, 4, 8
archaeology, 1-5
Auber, Harriet, **89**, 89

Baas manor, 10, 11, 16, 18, 20
Back, John, 58
Balfour, A.J., 87
Barclay Park, 96, **98**
Barclay, Joseph Gurney, 94
Barclay, Robert, 62, 74, 80, 82, 83, 87, 96
Basing House, 37, 38
Bassingbourne family, 8, **9**, 9, 18
Bassingbourne manor, 9, 13
Bassingbourne, Humphrey de, 13
Bassingbourne, John, 9, 18, 19
Bassingbourne, Thomas, 9, 18
Bayley, John, 25, **42**, 42
Beech Walk, 82, 96, **98**
Bell, **24**, 24, 25, **66**, 78
Bennet, James, 54
Bennet, John, 54
Bingley, Admiral Sir Alexander, 100
Bingley, Lady Juliet, 100
Birkett, George, 27, 29
Bisdee, Dr, **86**, 86
Black Death, 14
Bohun, de, **9**, 9, 13
Borham House, **77**, 77, 100
Borham, Esther (or Hester), 77
Borham, John, 48, 57
Borrell, John, **24**, 24, 42
Bosanquet, G.J., 66, 69
Bourchier, Anne, 20, 27
Bourchier, Henry, 12, 20
Bowle, Thomas, 27, 29
Boxe manor, 9, 11
Boxe, de, family, 9
Boxe, Richard de, 10, 12, 18

Bradshaws, 35, 78
brewery, 26, 52, 53, 58, **59**, 59, 61, 67, **90**, 90, 91
Briand, Kitty, 54
Briand, René, 53
British School, 72; Boys', **73**, 73, 81; Girls', 73, **74**, 74, 81, 98; Infants', 73, 74, 81
Brockett, Mary, 55
Bronze Age, 2
Broxbourne, 13, 14, 15, 20, 21, 27, 33, 34, 35, 40, 41, 43, 44, 45, 46, 47, 49, 68, 70, 105
Broxbourne, Borough of, 90, 96, 105
Broxbourne manor, 10
Broxbourne parish church. *See* St Augustine's, Broxbourne
Broxbournebury, 54
Broxbournebury manor, 7, 10, 31
Bull, **25**, 25, **41**, **64**, 64, **65**, 100
Burford House, 53, 87, 89
Burford House Academy, 87, **88**
Burford Street, 50, 62, 72, 90, 96
Bury, Richard de, 10, 11
bus service, 93

Cade, Jack, 17
Cathrow, George, 58, 62, 66
Cathrow, James, 69
Cecil, Robert, 1st Earl of Salisbury, 30, 40, 41, 42
Cecil, William, Lord Burghley, 20, **21**, 21, 22, 23, 24, 27, 29, 30
Cecil, William, 2nd Earl of Salisbury, 35, 36, 37, 38, 40
Cedar Green, 42, 99
cells, 14, 51, 62, 66
Celts, 2
Chamberleyne, Richard, 55
Chamberleyne, Stanes, 55
chapel, private, 52, **53**, 69
charity school, 72
Charlton Mill, 68
Cheffins, Caius, 64, 69
Cheffins, George, 55
Chekquers, 24, 25
Chertsey family, 11
Cheshunt, 1, 7, 8, 15, 21, 44, 47, 87, 96, 105
Chittenden, Reverend, 87
Christian, Edward, 83
Christie, Captain John Fairfax, 90

Christie, Charles Peter, 58, **59**, 59, 61, 67, 82, 96
Christie, Isabel, **61**, 61, 96
Christie, Peter, 58, 67
Christie, William, **58**, 58
Christ's Hospital Girls' School, 45
churches and chapels. *See* individual names
cinema, 90, **91**
Civic Hall, 92
Civil War, 35, 38, 39, 40, 42, 43, 47
Clock House (new), **66**, 66, 100
clock-house (old), **52**, 52, **66**, 66. *See also* St Katherine's chapel
Clock Tower, 100
Cock, 15, 21, 26, 35
Cock Lane, 2, 4, 5, 8, 21, 26, 28, 39, 82, 83, 94, 96
Cock, Sir Henry, 29, 31
Coffee Tavern, **79**, 79
Coffin Houses, **69**, 69. *See also* Yew Arbour
common field system, 7, 69
Congregational Church, 70, **74**, 80, 81, 100
court house, 41
Crown, 26

Danelaw, 5
Danes, 5, 6
Davies, Celia, 99
Dimsdale, Baron Thomas, 51
Dimsdale, Robert, 43, 51
Dobbs Weir, 8, 31, 68
Dolphin, 43, 50
Domesday, 7, 8, 11
Duke William of Cumberland, 100, **104**
Dymoke, John, 55

East, William, 70
Edeva the Fair, 7
education, 49, 70, 74, 81, 98. *See also* schools
Ellis, Sarah Stickney, 73, 80, **81**, 81, 82
Ellis, William, 73, 78, **80**, 80, 81
enclosure, 68
Ermine Street, 3, 4, 8, 12
Esdaile, James, 59
Esdaile House, **60**
Esdale House, 59, **60**, 99
Essex Road, 30, 48

fairs, 12, 13, 18, 27, 40, 66
Faithfull, Miss, 86
Faithfull, Mrs., 86, 87
Farringdon, 38
Fawkon on the Hoop, 15, 21, 33. *Also known as* Falcon on the Hoop
Fawkon Walk, 21, 74, 100
Feathers, 44
feudal system, 7, 12
fire engine, **51**, 51, 62, 66
First World War, 94
Five Horseshoes, 50, **62**, 62
Forres estate, 93, **94**
Fourways, 80, 81, 100, **104**
Foxton, Ralph de, 11
Foxtons manor, 10, 11, 16, 18
Frankland, Joyce, 30
Frankland, William, 24, 30

Fray, Sir John, 19, 20
Free Grammar School of Queen Elizabeth, 27, 29
Friends Meeting House, **48**, 48, 70, **72**

Game, William, 51
Gardiner, Thomas Murray, 89
Gardiner's Ironmongery, 89, **95**
gas works, 69, 93
Gedding, Edmund de, 11
Geddings manor, 11, 16, 18, 21, 61
George, 15, 24, 25, 26, 27, 80
Giddings, Charles, 96
Gode, 8, 9
Godes Well Acre, 36
Godith, 7, 8, 9
Golden Lion, **26**, 26
Goldingtons manor, 15
Gosse, Dr William, 84
Gosse, William Christie, **85**, 85
Gothic Cottages, 78, 100
Grange, 21, 26, 35, 39, **55**, 55, 56, 57, 58, 86, **87**, 87, 99
Great Amwell, 12, 13, 14, 15, 31, 32, 33, 34, 35, 40, 41, 43, 44, 52, 58, 70
Great Bed of Ware, 76
Green, Thomas, 54, 55, 56
Griffin, 21

Hailey, *xiii*, 12, 47, 75, 93
Hailey Hall, 52, 98
Hailey manor, 8, 10, 15, 16, 30, 98
Hallmores, 26
Hallow, Miss, 54
Hargraves, Edward, 87
Harold II (Godwinson), 6, 7, 8
Harris, Elizabeth, 77, 78
Harteshorne, 26
Haselwoood, W., 87
Haslewood School, 98
Hassall, Thomas, 31, 34, 35, 40, 41, 43, 44, 64
Hertford, 1, 4, 5, 6, 12, 18, 19, 27, 45, 54, 62, 74
Hertford Heath, 4, 12, 33, 62
High Leigh, 3, 61, 82, **83**, 96, **97**
High Pavement, 102
High Street, **63**, **64**, **65**, 66, **85**, **101**, **104**
highway robbery, 62
Hoddesdon Chapel, **70**, 70
Hoddesdon House, 35. *See also* Rawdon House
Hoddesdon manor, 9, 10
Hoddesdon parish, 52, 70
Hoddesdon parish church. *See* chapel, private; Hoddesdon Chapel; St Catherine's church; St Catherine & St Paul's church; St Paul's church
Hoddesdon Park Wood, 9
Hoddesdonbury, **100**, 100
Hoddesdonbury manor, 4, 8, 9, 13, 14, 18, 19, 20, 21, 22, 27
Hogges Hall, 9, **10**
Hoole, John, 54
Horley, Dr. William, 85
hospital, 14, **15**, 15, 20, 27, 29, 33
Hughes family, 57, 87
Hughes, Hugh, 57
Hummerstone, Sarah, 77, 78
Hunt, John, 70, 74

Hunt, Robert, 58, 73
Hunts, builders, 105

ice ages, 1
Independent Chapel, 80, **81**
inns, public houses, hotels, 24-26. *See also* individual names
Iron Age, 1, 2
Italian Cottage. *See* Spinning Wheel

James, Dr, 61
John Warner School, 98
Jones, Mrs Easter, 72
Jones, Reverend William, 58

Keeling, Joseph, 53
Keeling, William, 22, 23, 24
Kempe, Misses, 80
King's Arms, 74

Lampit Field, 29, 68
Lampits, **68**, 68, **103**
Langton family, 11
Langtons manor, 9, 11, 18
Lea valley, 1, 2, 3, 7, 54
Lea, river, *xiv*, 1, 3, 4, 5, 6, 12, 18, 29, 31, 54, 57
Lee Valley Regional Park, 93
Lee, priest of St Catherine's Chapel, 13, 14
Lee, river, *xiii, xiv*
Leigh, Lord, 56
leprosy, 14, 15
library, 94, **95**, 95, 96
Limesi, Ralph de, 9, 10, 11
Little Ice Age, 31, 44
local government, 45, 69, 105
Lord Street, 8, 43, 59, 66, **67**, 72, 80, 82, 86
Lowewood, **56**, 57, **77**, 77, 79, 94, 95
Lowewood Museum, 45, 69, 95, 96
Lynch Mill, 22, 29, 57, **68**, 68
Lynch, The, 29, 30, 33, 57, 68, **103**

McAdam, John Loudon, 86
McKenzie, Alexander, 69
Maidenhead, 13, **26**, 26, **65**, **66**, 100, 102
malt, 29, 30
Mandeville, de, **9**
Mandeville, Geoffrey de, 9
manor courts, 14, 45, 69
manors, 7-11. *See also* individual manors
Manser, Alfred, 68
Manser, Edward, 68
Manser, Harold, 69
Manser, James Poulter, 68, 69
Marche, William de la, 13, 26
market, 12, 13, 18, 19, 27, 29, 30, 40, 41, 62, 64, **65**, 66, 67, 93
market cross, 12, 13, 19, 44, 64
market house, 40, **41**, 41, 44, 64, **65**
Marsh Lane, 30, 48, 70
marshes, 7, 11, 69, 84
maypole, 62
meads, 7, 68, 69
Middle Class Academy, **88**, 89

Middle Row, **64**, **65**, **66**, 67
Mitchell family, 41
Mitchell, Robert, 14, 41
Molesworth, Bevill, 35
Molesworth, Martha, 35
Montague House, **86**, 86
Morice, Reverend William, 71, 73
museum. *See* Lowewood Museum
Myddelton, Hugh, 32

National School, 72, 74, **99**; Boys', **70**, 72, **73**, 96; Girls', 72, **73**, 73, 98; Infants', 73
New River, **32**, 32, **33**, 33, 36
New River Company, 33, 69
Newport Grammar School, 30
Nissen huts, 94, **95**
Norman Conquest, 7
Norris Lodge, 59, **86**, 86, 99
North, Sara, 39
nurse children, 32

O'Brien, Admiral Donat Henchy, **84**, 84
Oddo, 8
Ogard family, 15, 17, 30
Ogard, Andrew, 15, 16, 17
Ogard, George, 30
Ogard, Henry, 17
Oxendon, Lady Arabella, 55, 56

Paddick, E.W., 95
Pank, Martha, 48, 57
parish constable, 14, 29, 45
Parish of Hoddesdon. *See* Hoddesdon parish
Parr, William, 20
Pauls Lane, 3, 73, 96, 98
Pepys, Samuel, 45
pest-house, 61
plague, 31, 44
Plomer, Robert, 50, 52, 53
Plomer, William, 52
police, 45, 66, 92
police station, 35, 66, **67**, 100
poverty and the poor, 4, 14, 15, 20, 23, 27, 29, 30, 31, 32, 33, 35, 45, 46, 49, 50, 51, 61, 62, 72
pre-history, 1
Pulham & Son, 78, 82, 83
Pulham, James, 78

Quakers. *See* Society of Friends
Queen Victoria Cottage Homes, 62
quern, 4, **5**, 5, 8

railways, 67, 68, 69, 74, 76
Rathmore House, **57**, 57, **60**, 61, 84
Rawdon family, 31, **34**, **36**, 35-40, 41, 53
Rawdon House, 35, 36, **37**, 38, 40, 52, 55, 59, 78, 79, 81, **82**, 82, **99**, 99; water supply, 35, 39, 40, 42
Rawdon, Elizabeth, 26, **34**, 35, 36, 40
Rawdon, Hester, 52
Rawdon, Marmaduke (grandson of Sir Marmaduke), 26, 40
Rawdon, Marmaduke (second son of Sir Marmaduke), 36, 38, **39**, 39, 56

Rawdon, Marmaduke (the Traveller), 36, 38, **39**, 39
Rawdon, Sir Marmaduke, 35-38, **37**, 41, 52
Rawdon, Thomas, 36, **38**, 38
Red Lion, 43
Ricardo, Henry, 82
Rich, Richard, 15, 25, 61
road repairs, 15, 20, 31, 86
Roman Catholic Church, St Augustine's, 99, 100
Roman era, 2-4
Roman Street, 3, 5
Rosehill, 78, **80**, 80, 81, 94
Rumbold, Richard, 47, 48
Rye Common, 69, 74
Rye House, *xiii*, 12, 15-17, **16**, 30, 45, **47**, 47, **61**, 62, 74, **76**, 76, 90, 91, **92**, 92, 105
Rye House Hotel, **76**, 76
Rye House Plot, **47**, 47
Rye manor, 8, 10, 15, 17, 30
Rye Park, *xiii*, 69, 74, 75, 93, 105

St Augustine's church, Broxbourne, 13, 19, 20, 24, 33, 35, 42, 45, 52, 55
St Catherine's church, 70, **71**
St Catherine & St Paul's church, **53**, 96
St Cuthbert's church, 74, **93**, 93
St George, 25
St Katherine's chapel, 13, 14, 34, 41, 44, 51, 52, 57. *See also* clock house (old)
St Margarets, 12, 54
St Monica's Priory, 82, 99. *See also* Rawdon House
St Paul's church, 96, **97**
Salisbury Arms, **24**, 25, 69, 93
Salisbury, Marquess of, 64, 69, 87, 93
Samaritan Woman, **40**, 40, **63**, 64, **96**, 96
Sarmoners manor, 10, 11
Saxey, William, 30
Say family, 17-20, **19**
Say, Agnes, 19
Say, Elizabeth, **17**, 17, 18, 19
Say, Katherine, 18
Say, Sir John, 11, **17**, 17-19
Say, Sir William (son of Sir John), 15, 19, 20
Say, William (brother of Sir John), 11, 17
schools, 27, 29, 30, 41, 45, 50, 54, **70**, 72, **73**, 73, **74**, 74, 79, 81, 82, 83, 85, 87, 89, 96, 98, 99. *See also* individual schools
Scott, John, 54
Second World War, 94-95
Sharnbrooke family, 25
Sharnbrooke, William (Jnr & Snr), 27
Sheredes Comprehensive School, 98
Simmons, Thomas, 77
smallpox, 50, 54, 61
Society of Friends, 48, 73, 77
Spinning House, 30, 49
Spinning Wheel, **79**, 79
Spital Brook, 7, 8, 14, 27, 83
Spitalbrook, 26, 78, 86, 89
Stanboroughs, 41, **42**, **85**, 85, 99
street lighting, 69, 93
street names, *xiv*
Sunday school, 50, 83

Taylor, Douglas, 95
Teale, Henry, 74, 76
Thatched House, **44**, 44, 52, 59
Thele manor, 11, 15, 16, 30
Theobalds, 21
Thorowgood family, **25**, 33-35
Thorowgood, Elizabeth, 26, 35. *See also* Rawdon, Elizabeth
Thorowgood, John (cousin of William), 21-24
Thorowgood, Martha, 35. *See also* Molesworth, Martha
Thorowgood, Thomas (d. 1576/7), 21, 27
Thorowgood, Thomas (d. 1615), 21, 26, 34, 35
Thorowgood, William (d. 1602), 21, 23, 26, 29, 33, 34, 35
Thurgoods, 26
toll road, 12, 17, 45
Tower Centre, 100, **103**, **104**
Town House, 40
turnpike, 86
Tutty, Mrs, 54

Urban District of Hoddesdon, 69, 93, 95, 100, 105

vagrancy, 30, 32, 51, 62, 66
vestry, 45, 49, 50, 51, 55

Waller, E., 87
Walmsley, Miss, 84
war memorial, 94
Ware, 3, 4, 29, 54, 61
Ware Workhouse Union, 62
Warner, Celia, 79
Warner, Charles Borham, 79
Warner, Elizabeth Ann, 94
Warner, Harriette, 79
Warner, John, 57, 73, 77-79, **78**
Warner, John Jnr, 79
Warner, Mary, 79, 94
Warner, Robert, 87
Warner, Sarah, 78
Warner, Septimus, 79
watercress, **68**, 68, 103
waterworks, 69
weathervane, **67**, 67
Webb, Charles, 69, 82
White Hart, 44
White Swan, **24**, 24, 25
Whitley Road, 59, 61, 74, 93
Whitley, Charles (Jnr & Snr), 69
Whitley, Charles S., 95
Whittingstall, E.W., 69
Whittingstall, Mrs, 87
Whittingstall, William, 53, 58
Williams, Admiral William Peere, 83
woodland and woods, 3, 9, 10, 21-24, 27, 29, 36, 38, 40, 105
Woodlands, 35, **78**, 78, 79, **100**, 100
Worcester Militia, 54
workhouse, 50, 61, 62
Wulfwin, 8, 10

Yew Arbour, **69**, 69, 105. *Also known as* The Coffin Houses
Yew House, 24, 41, 42, 54, 83, **84**, 84, 93
Yewlands, 93

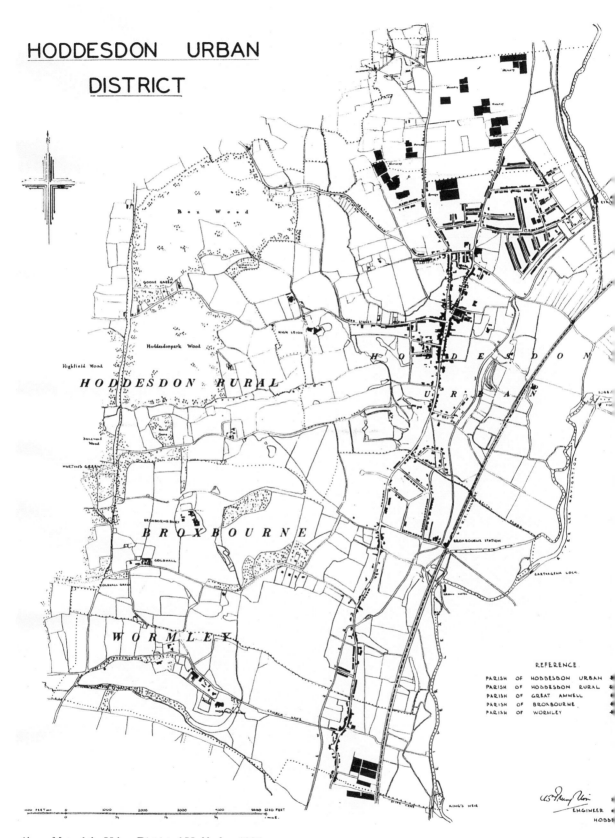

HODDESDON URBAN DISTRICT

Box Wood

GOOSE GREEN

Hoddesdonpark Wood

HIGH LEIGH

Highfield Wood

HODDESDON RURAL

Danemead Wood

MARTINS GREEN

Grove

BROXBOURNEBURY

BROXBOURNE

COLDHALL

COLDHALL GREEN

KING'S WEIR

BROXBOURNE STATION

CARTHAGENA LOCK

GROVE HOTEL

WORMLEY

WORMLEY BURY

CHURCH LANE

1000 FEET   0   1000   2000   3000   4000   5000   6000 FEET

ENGINEER

HODDE

Above: Map of the Urban District of Hoddesdon, 1936.
Right: Map of principal buildings and roads in and around Hoddesdon, 1988. © P. E. Rooke